No Other Foundation
Essays on Women's Ordination in the Anglican Church

THE STATE OF THE QUESTION AFTER FIFTY YEARS

EDITED BY

Ben Jefferies

The North American Anglican Press

Omaha, Nebraska

NO OTHER FOUNDATION
Essays on Women's Ordination in the Anglican Church

Edited by Ben Jefferies

The authors of these essays hold the copyrights individually.

E.L. Mascall 'Women Priests?' (Second Edition) published by *Church Literature Association* (June 1977), and re-issued by *Forward in Faith Scotland* (1998). C.S. Lewis 'Priestesses in the Church?' originally published as 'Notes on the Way,' in *Time and Tide* (1948). A. Linsley 'Ten Objections to Women Priests' originally published online by *Virtue Online* (Nov 2019). B. Jefferies' 'Holy Orders and Authentein', and 'Holy Orders and Prophets' originally published online by *The North American Anglican* (Feb 2020) and revised for this publication. L. Nelson's 'The Problem with Making a Pro-WO Patristic Argument' originally published online by *Anglican Compass* (Nov 2019). A. Wilgus' 'Imago Dei, Persona Christi' originally published online by *The North American Anglican* (Nov 2019). B. Johnson 'Sacramental Representation and the Created Order' originally published online by *Theopolis Institute* (Nov 2019). B. Jefferies 'Brothers, We Have Failed' originally published online by *Anglican Compass* (Feb 2020). G. McDermott 'God is Not Fair' originally published by *Anglican Compass* (Jan 2020).

Although sincere effort has been made to trace and contact copyright holders prior to publication, this has not been possible in every case. If notified the publishers will be pleased to rectify any errors or omissions at the earliest opportunity.

This publication ©2021
The North American Anglican Press
Omaha, Nebraska

The North American Anglican Press is a department of The North American Anglican, LLC. It furthers entity's object of excellence in research, ressourcement, and the renaissance of both Christian theology and the arts within the Anglican tradition.

Cover Design and Type-Setting by Ben Jefferies

ISBN 978-1-7359230-1-7

TABLE OF CONTENTS

INTRODUCTION

HOW DID WE GET HERE?

Women Priests? | *E.L. Mascall*   5

WHAT'S THE BIG PICTURE?

Priestesses in the Church? | *C.S. Lewis*   43
Ten Objections to Women Priests | *A. Linsley*   53

WHAT'S THE LATEST ON THE LOCI CLASSICI?

Holy Orders and *Authentein* (1 Timothy 2:12) | *B. Jefferies*   67
Holy Orders and Prophets (1 Corinthians 11 & 14) | *B. Jefferies*   81

WHAT IS STILL AT STAKE, SYMBOLICALLY?

The Problem with Making a Pro-WO Patristic Argument | *L. Nelson*   97
Imago Dei, Persona Christi | *A. Wilgus*   111
Sacramental Representation and the Created Order | *B. Johnson*   119

HOW SHOULD THIS BE PRESENTED, PASTORALLY?

Brothers, We Have Failed | *B. Jefferies*   127
God is Not Fair | *G. McDermott*   135

WHERE DO WE GO FROM HERE?

The Way Back | *C. Findley*   141

INTRODUCTION

The ordination of women to the priesthood is not a settled question. Though women have been (nominally) ordained to the priesthood within North America for nearly fifty years, the mere passage of time has not settled the question of whether or not Women's Ordination (WO) has been in keeping with God's will as presented in his Word. Despite the hegemony of the women's movement in the culture at large, fifty years later it is still the case that pro-WO scholars and theologians have not settled the question in the eyes of the wider church either. The fact that pro-WO books continue to be written and published seventy years into the discussion *ipso facto* proves this fact, as does the existence of "dual integrities" within the Anglican Church in North America. Both sides contend that "dual integrities" is an oxymoron in need of resolution one way or the other.

A new inquirer into the question at hand, biased by a gender-neutralizing zeitgeist, might read a pro-WO text and think that the argument is well made, and that only "curmudgeons" who can't "get with the times" would think otherwise. However, as these collected essays evidence, a closer inspection of the arguments that underwrite the opposition to WO — biblical, theological, anthropological, pastoral — reveals that many clear and weighty points have been side-stepped rather than answered. The collection of these essays is intended to be a "text-book" of sorts, to keep these arguments before the eyes of the present generation of Anglicans.

E.L. Mascall's essay catalogues the development of the pro-WO case in the Church of England, which very closely resembles the history in the United States in its prioritization of a program ahead of real *theological* engagement, which Mascall then supplies.

C.S.Lewis' seminal essay 'Priestesses in the Church' remains a touch-stone for deep theological thinking (it is quoted by Mascall) to this day. Pre-empting John Paul II's theology of the body by several decades, he shines light on the essential role of gender in God's creative and redemptive work without reducing the case to gender essentialism.

Alice Linsley's essay is something of a bridge between the mid 20th century and the present, as she catalogues the ways in which confusion about gender in the priesthood has precipitated all manner of theological and practical disasters in the Church in the years since the ordination of women to the priesthood began.

The remaining essays were written in the past year (2019-2020) and most of them were first published online. These essays telescope the perennial theological issues into the midst of the Anglican Church today; repristinating the strong arguments of the past, with an eye to how the debates have shifted in the intervening decades.

The composite case made in these essays still awaits a satisfactory answer; there has been much debate these past fifty years, but the fact remains that no other foundation can be laid except that which has been laid (1 Cor 3:11) by our Lord Jesus himself: a male priesthood.

—Ben Jefferies
CONFESSION OF ST. PETER 2021

WOMEN PRIESTS?

E. L. Mascall

1977

PRELIMINARIES

In discussing whether women should be ordained to the priesthood or not it will be well, for the sake of clarity, to make some preliminary points.

First of all, it must be recognised that two quite distinct questions are involved, though once their common existence and their mutual distinctness have been accepted it will for the most part be possible to discuss them together. The former is whether it is *possible* for women to be priests, the latter is whether it is *right and desirable* for them to be priests; and unless the former is answered in the affirmative the second cannot arise. This is important, because it is frequently assumed without argument that a woman upon whom the traditional rites of ordination to the priesthood have been performed by a bishop will undoubtedly have become a priest, so that the only questions remaining to be discussed are ethical ones (Is it not unjust to withhold the priesthood from women?) and pastoral ones (Will not women perform the traditional duties and functions of the priesthood just as efficiently as men?).

Secondly – and this is closely connected with the first point – it must be stressed that what we are concerned with is the Catholic priesthood, as that has come down to us in the great episcopal communions of East and West, and not with the various forms of ministry that exist in the Protestant churches and communities. In saying this, one is not adopting an attitude of contempt or unfriendliness to our separated brethren but simply recognising the fact that the Catholic conception of the ministry is different from the Protestant conception, even if the Catholic conception includes the Protestant conception as an element in itself, and even if – as is undoubtedly the case – the Catholic conception is itself undergoing today a great deal of re-examination and development. We shall see later on that on one understanding of the nature of the ministry in Protestantism the ordination of women is no less abhorrent than it is in traditional Catholicism and Orthodoxy. It is indeed doubtful whether there is one basic doctrine of the ministry held throughout Protestantism, of which the views of the different denominations are merely variants. When, for example, the late Paul Tillich wrote: "There are in Protestantism only laymen; the minister is a layman with a special function within the congregation . . . . He is a non-layman solely by virtue of his training," he was not merely contradicting himself verbally by saying first that a minister is a layman and then that he is not; he was expressing a view of the ministry quite contrary to that of many Protestants, who would hold that what makes a minister is neither his training nor his choice by a congregation but his call by God. The point remains that, on Tillich's view and no doubt on some other Protestant views as well, there is nothing impossible in a woman becoming a minister, for she is just as capable of undergoing a course of training as a man. I must add that I do not despair, as ecumenical dialogue proceeds, of Catholics and Protestants coming to a common understanding of the Church's ministry. What I do maintain is that they have not come to it yet, and that discussions about the ordination of women, as of other matters connected with the ministry, frequently reach a condition of frustration through lack of agreement about what the ministry is and sometimes through the lack of any clear conception about the ministry at all.

This point can be illustrated by the decision of the established Church of Scotland to open its ministry in principle to women. This was announced by the newspapers, no doubt in accordance with the tenor of the preceding debates in the General Assembly, under such headlines as "Pulpits now open to Women" and "Women now allowed to preach". Now I do not deny the importance of preaching as a function of the ordained minister nor do I suggest that Presbyterian ministers never celebrate the sacraments, but it will, I think, be clear that the nature of the debate and the grounds of decision are likely to be very different in a church in which sermons are preached every Sunday but the Lord's Supper is usually celebrated only once a quarter from what they will be in a church in which the Holy Eucharist is celebrated weekly or even daily. In the former case the primary question will be "Should women be commissioned to preach the word of God?", in the latter it will be "Should (or can) women be ordained to celebrate the Eucharist?", and it will be well to bear this difference in mind when consulting such statistics as those given in a recent number of *Concilium* about the practice of various churches in the matter, since it is logically possible to give an affirmative answer to the former question and a negative one to the latter.

It is furthermore important not to misunderstand the suggestions, (in some cases even the demands) emanating from certain Roman Catholic circles for the ordination of women to the priesthood. Some of these rest upon no theological basis at all and are merely typical of a temperamental desire to destroy all the inherited structures of the Church and to assimilate the Catholic religion to the trends and outlooks of the contemporary secularised world. Some of them, however, manifest a praiseworthy wish to give the Church's life a wider and firmer foundation than that of post-Tridentine scholasticism. It is important to remember that it is a common practice in the Roman Catholic Church to question the truth of a statement or the legitimacy of a practice in order to elicit the fundamental reasons for the truth or the real grounds of the practice; thus, to give a famous example, St. Thomas Aquinas in the *Summa Theologiae* raised without qualms the question whether God exists. In a communion in which nothing is likely to be upset overnight there is a lot to be said for this method; it is well exemplified by the resolution which was submitted by Cardinal Flahiff to the Synod of Bishops in Rome in October, 1971, on behalf of the bishops of Canada, urging the immediate establishment of a mixed commission to study in depth the question of the ministries [sic] of women in the Church. While it was understood that this did not exclude the question of the priesthood (and in deed no comprehensive study could), it was emphasised that there was no desire to prejudge the question or to make recommendations as to time or mode of further action. There is thus no justification for Anglicans to urge such Roman stirrings as providing an example for precipitate imitation, or for saying "Rome is going to ordain women, so let us get in first". This is not, however, the first case in which the tentative reopening of a question by Roman Catholic bishops or theologians has been taken by over-enthusiastic Anglicans as an invitation to jettison traditional positions of doctrine or practice.

THE STATE OF THE QUESTION

In assessing the present situation it is perhaps well to recall that in 1962, following the publication of a report with the rather odd title *Gender and Ministry* (odd because "gender" has usually been taken as a grammatical and not an anthropological term) which had been prepared by a working-party of the Central Advisory Council on Training for the Ministry (CACTM), the Church Assembly requested the Archbishops of Canterbury and York "to appoint a Committee to make a thorough examination of the various reasons for the withholding of the ordained and representative priesthood from women". In response to this the two Archbishops appointed a Commission with the simpler terms of reference "to examine the question of Women and Holy Orders". This Commission produced a report which was published in December, 1966, under the title *Women and Holy Orders*. It refrained, probably wisely, from making any recommendations but confined itself to assembling a large amount of historical material and setting out the arguments which had been urged both for and against the ordination of women to the priesthood. In July, 1967, the Church Assembly rejected a resolution welcoming the further consideration of the matter by the Advisory Council for the Church's Ministry (ACCM, the successor of CACTM), the Council for Women's Ministry in the Church and the Joint Committee of Representatives of the Church of England and the Methodist Church and describing itself as "believing that there are no conclusive theological reasons why women should not be ordained to the priesthood but recognising that it would not be wise to take unilateral action at this time". The Methodist Conference, the supreme governing body of the Methodist Church in this country, had already, in 1966, affirmed its conviction "that women may properly be ordained to the Ministry of the Word and Sacraments" but, "recognising that it would not be wise to take unilateral action at this time", expressed a desire for discussions with representatives of the Church of England. This discussion took place and its results were published in May, 1968, under the title *Women and the Ordained Ministry*. With an eye on the Anglican/Methodist union scheme this report expressed the view that unilateral action by the Methodist Church would not be an insurmountable barrier to Stage One of the Scheme but, unless the Church of England had decided to ordain women, might well hinder the implementation of Stage Two.

This piece of domestic history can have been of little direct interest to most of the members of the 1968 Lambeth Conference, but the general question must have been present to their minds. The subcommittee on Women and the Priesthood, while expressing great respect for the opposite view, came down unhesitatingly in support of the ordination of women; it found "no conclusive theological reasons for withholding ordination to the priesthood from women as such". It did indeed assert:

> The appeal to Scripture and tradition deserves to be taken with the utmost seriousness. To disregard what we have received from the apostles, and the inheritance of Catholic Christendom, would be most inappropriate for a Church for which the authority of Scripture and tradition stands high.

Nevertheless, the appeal to Scripture was dismissed by juxtaposing two passages from St. Paul, one of which would, if anything, count against the ordination of women while the other has no explicit relevance to it. Similarly, the appeal to tradition was dismissed without detailed argument on biological and sociological grounds. It was added that "the element of sexuality in the Godhead and its implication for the sex of the priesthood are complex and debatable matters", but the sub-committee felt itself competent to solve these complex and debatable matters in nine lines. The rest of the sub-committee's report makes no reference to matters of principle but contents itself with asserting that churches which have ordained women have been satisfied with the results.

It is difficult to discover whether the matter received really adequate discussion in the crowded and hurried conditions of the Conference's full sessions. In Resolution 34 it "affirm[ed] its opinion that the theological arguments as at present presented for and against the ordination of women to the priesthood are inconclusive". The addition of the words "or against" might seem significant. The Conference made it plain, however, in its subsequent resolutions that this state of alleged theological inconclusiveness was not to be taken seriously and that action could be envisaged on the assumption that the arguments *against* were valueless and that only the arguments *for* were valid. It asked all the parts of the Anglican Communion to give careful study to the question and to report their findings to the Anglican Consultative Council (ACC), which would make them generally available. The ACC was also asked to initiate consultations with other Churches, both those which did and those which did not ordain women, and distribute the information thus secured. The Conference also requested that any Anglican national or regional Church or province contemplating ordaining women to the priesthood should seek and carefully consider the advice of the ACC (Resolutions 35–37). This last request is indeed surprising, for in it the Bishops of the Anglican Communion were shifting their responsibility, in a major matter affecting the basic structure of the Church, to a body of somewhat haphazard constitution which at the time of Lambeth 1968, had not even come into existence. When the ACC in fact came into existence and met in February and March, 1971, at Limuru in Kenya it consisted of fifty-one persons, bishops, priests and lay-people, each of the member churches of the Anglican Communion contributing two or three. The only *ex officio* member was the Archbishop of Canterbury. In spite of Resolution 37 of Lambeth 1968, it is difficult to see that advising about the ordination of women falls within the eight functions which Lambeth itself assigned to the ACC when it constituted it in Resolution 69. It is certainly difficult to see that all the members of the ACC had the necessary qualifications to consider such a matter in more than a pragmatic or emotional way. However, even setting such doubts aside, the resolution, No. 28(b), which was passed at Limuru has some very peculiar features. It was passed by 24 votes to 22 in the following terms:

> In reply to the request of the Council of the Church of Southeast Asia, this Council advises the Bishop of Hong Kong, acting with the approval of his Synod, and any other bishop of the Anglican Communion acting with the approval of his Province, that, if he decides to ordain women to the priesthood, his action will be acceptable to this Council; and that this Council will use its good offices to encourage all Provinces of the Anglican Communion to continue in communion with these dioceses.

There is a very serious ambiguity about the phrase "this Council" in this resolution. Does it mean the fifty-one persons present at Limuru from February 23rd to March 5th, 1971, or does it include any future meetings of the ACC? If the former, it is impossible for "this Council" to use its good offices or do anything else after the latter of these dates, since it will then no longer exist, and if it is suggested that the individual members will find the proposed action acceptable and use their good offices, this is very doubtful, since just under half the members voting did in fact vote against the resolution. If, on the other hand, "this Council" is intended to include future meetings of the Council, with, in all probability, a largely different membership, the resolution is surely *ultra vires*, since no authority has been given to the members of the ACC in 1971 to bind their successors for ever and it would need a shift of only two votes for the resolution to be rescinded. No one, I think, has suggested that decisions of the ACC, like *ex cathedra* papal pronouncements, are irreformable of themselves and not by the consent of the Church. And indeed it would seem rash in the extreme for any part of the

Anglican Communion to rely upon such fragile and tenuous assurances. This is not just a debating point, but involves a matter of serious principle. Have the bishops of the Anglican Communion handed over their responsibility in the matter of the ordination of women to a bare majority of such an amorphous and fluctuating assembly as the Anglican Consultative Council?

At least one bishop appears to think so, for on Advent Sunday, 1971, the Bishop of Hong Kong went through the form of ordaining two women to the priesthood, in spite of the fact that the Archbishop of Canterbury had asked that no bishop should so act before all the Anglican provinces had stated their views. His Grace had been quoted several times as saying that ordination of women to the priesthood would ultimately come but that the time had not yet arrived; clearly the Bishop of Hong Kong disagreed on this latter point and saw no reason to accept the Archbishop's plea for delay. In any case, the ACC at Limuru, in Resolution 28(a), has asked all the Anglican Churches to express their views in time for its next meeting in 1973, so there would seem to be, at any rate in the ACC's own opinion, some urgency in the matter.

SCRIPTURE AND TRADITION

In any other matter than this the argument from Scripture and Tradition would be considered overwhelming. The words which I have quoted above from the Lambeth sub-committee could hardly have been stronger:

> The appeal to Scripture and tradition deserves to be taken with the utmost seriousness. To disregard what we have received from the apostles, and the inheritance

of Catholic Christendom, would be most inappropriate for a Church for which the authority of Scripture and tradition stands high.

This, one might think, would have disposed of the matter. It is therefore little less than astonishing to find the sub-committee dismissing both Scripture and tradition in two brief paragraphs in a way that, by its own standards, is most inappropriate and which certainly does not manifest the utmost seriousness. All that is said about Scripture is this:

> Nevertheless the data of Scripture appear to be divided on this issue. St. Paul's insistence on female subordination, made to enforce good order in the anarchy at Corinth, is balanced by his declaration in Gal. 3, 28, that in the one Christ there is no distinction of Jew against Gentile, slave against free man, male against female.

That is all – not a word about the highly theological exposition in Ephesians V, in which the relation of man to woman is compared with that of Christ to the Church, and not a word about the attitude and teaching of Christ himself. Those who advocate the ordination of women usually start from the undeniable fact that, whereas in Judaism women occupy an essentially inferior position, if for no other reason that they are physically unable to be admitted into the Covenant by the rite of circumcision, in Christianity the water of baptism and the unction of the Spirit are available indifferently to men and women alike. The bearing of the argument is, however, all the other way. For it is the same primitive Church which is appealed to as witnessing to the absolute equality of all Christians, both male and female, in their status as members of the Body of Christ through baptism, which restricted the

Church's ministerial functions to men. Behind the action of the Church in this matter there lies the example of her Founder, who (as we see for example in his condemnation of the Jewish attitude to divorce) was full of sympathy for women but who nevertheless founded the Church's ministry by giving it a purely male apostolate. It would be absurd to suppose that in doing this Christ was depriving women of their legitimate rights, and misleading his Church as to their true status, as a concession to the conventions and prejudices of the time; even his enemies never accused him of conventionality and cowardice and it would ill become his disciples in the twentieth century to do so. When we find our Lord and the primitive Church restricting the ministry to males in spite of the emphasis laid by both alike on the absolute equality of men and women as members of the New Israel which is the Body of Christ, is it not prudent to assume that there must be some very deep and significant reason in the nature of things for this restriction?

The following paragraphs from the chapter on the Case against the Ordination of Women to the Priesthood in the report *Women and Holy Orders* deserve to be quoted at length; nothing in the subsequent chapter putting the opposite case seems to me to answer them:

(a) It would be contrary to the tradition of the Church, from the time of the Apostles. If it is to be maintained that that tradition is wrong it has to be demonstrated, either that the Apostles failed to divine or to implement the intention of Christ, if he intended women to partake in the priestly ministry, or that Christ erred in not declaring this to be his intention. Neither proposition can validly be maintained. It is therefore quite legitimate to assert that the exclusion of women from Holy Orders is just part of the nature of things, in this case of the nature of the Christian Church.

(b) The conviction that the priesthood can only be male is supported by the deliberate inclusion by Christ and the Apostles of women with men in the wider priesthood of the whole Church. There is a general priesthood of the whole people of God, comprising men and women, and a specific priesthood of those who have been ordained to it. The wider priesthood of the Laos indicates that if the ministerial priesthood is composed only of males, this is in the divine ordinance as much as the existence of the Church itself. If only secondary difficulties stood in the way, the ministry could easily have been opened to both sexes.

(c) Allied to this argument is that based on the recognition that Christianity was a revolutionary religion, not least in the greatly heightened esteem and value accorded to women . . . . The maleness or the Christian priesthood must therefore have deeper grounds than mere conservatism or a poor estimate of the feminine nature.

(d) All theistic religions (that is to say, religions in which the God or Gods transcend the created order and stand behind nature and history, as well as acting in them, rather than being merged in a monistic or pantheistic unity) have male priesthoods. Female priesthoods belong to the nature religions in which human nature is sensed to be merely part of society, society part of nature, and nature itself Divine. The Christian Church, rooted in the biblical view of God and his relation to the world, has without question adopted a male priesthood. It is therefore pertinent to ask whether the feature of a male priesthood can be modified by the addition of a female priesthood without altering the essential character of the Christian ministry, and without affecting the human psyche at those deep levels at which it responds to religious symbolism.

None of these considerations appears to have made any impression on the Lambeth sub-committee, which indeed shows no signs of having heard of them. After the summary dismissal of Scripture to which I have referred above, it deals with tradition as follows:

> It appears that the *tradition* flowing from the early Fathers and the medieval Church that a woman is incapable of receiving Holy Orders reflects biological assumptions about the nature of woman and her relation to man which are considered unacceptable in the light of modern knowledge and biblical study and have been generally discarded today. If the ancient and medieval assumptions about the social role and inferior status of women are no longer accepted, the appeal to tradition is virtually reduced to the observation that there happens to be no precedent for ordaining women to be priests. The New Testament does not encourage Christians to think that nothing should be done for the first time.

In the absence of any details it is difficult to assess the force of these references to biology and sociology, but in order to make a case for the abandonment of the unvarying tradition of the Church we should need answers to the following questions: (1) What, if any, were the false biological views in question? (2) How did it follow from them that women could not be ordained to the priesthood? (3) What are the views which have taken their place? (4) Do those views imply that women *can* be ordained to the priesthood? (5) In what ways were women in the past believed to be socially inferior? (6) Did this belief imply that women could not be ordained to the priesthood and if so, how? (7) Have the views about women which have now come to be held been proved to be true? (8) If so, do they imply that women can be ordained to the priesthood? All these are serious questions and the matter is not to be dealt with by casual reference to biology and sociology. Even if the refusal to ordain women in the past rested on a false belief in their inferiority (and it is doubtful whether this has been proved), there may still be other reasons against their ordination. In any case I would suggest that all this talk about inferiority and inequality is really irrelevant and un-Christian. For the basic fact about the sexes is not that they are inferior or superior to each other but that they are different.

THE DIFFERENCE OF THE SEXES

Supporters of the ordination of women frequently point to the alleged injustice of the exclusion of one half of the human race from the status and functions of priesthood. There will be something to say later about this assumption that priesthood is a status that can be possessed as a right, but it may be relevant to remark that there is already a status and function from which one half of the human race is constitutionally and incurably excluded, namely that of motherhood. And if it is true that the order of redemption is not isolated from the order of creation and that grace does not ignore or destroy nature but presupposes and perfects it, it would be very strange if the differentiation of function on the level of nature was not paralleled by a not less marked differentiation of function on the level of grace. One of the results of the modern tendency to emphasise the idea of equality rather than that of differentiation is the type of feminism which by demanding the same functions for women as for men implicitly assumes the superiority of male status. If women want to be as like men as possible, this can only mean that manhood is essentially superior to womanhood. This is not a view that any Christian should accept; its basic absurdity is seen in the recent demand by a member of the Women's Liberation Movement that women should refuse to bear babies any more and that scientists should immediately perfect the technique of growing babies in test-tubes.

The chapter in *Women and Holy Orders* from which I have previously quoted makes this point clearly and with restraint:

(e) The assertion that the ordination of women is the logical outcome of a steadily growing recognition of woman's full humanity is fallacious. A philosophy of social evolution making for this kind of equivalence of women with men has no backing in historical, philosophical, biological or religious theory.

(f) Western civilisation has witnessed a hypertrophy, a morbid enlargement, of its masculine aptitudes, and the feminist movement, by bringing women into the characteristic masculine way of handling life, has aggravated the disease. The characteristics of the two sexes must be regarded as complementary. In the concrete, for the art of living, there are male and female aptitudes. A refusal to recognise this polarity of the sexes tends to create not satisfaction, but further and more deep-seated restlessness.

(g) The view that sex is irrelevant in deciding who should or should not be ordained to the priesthood has been based on a belief that there is a sexless human nature common to men and women underlying their sex differences. This view is no longer tenable. There is in fact a masculine and a feminine human nature with some complication from the shadow of the opposite sex in each.

Like other advocates of female emancipation, the proponents of the ordination of women are not always consistent in their arguments, which oscillate between at least three positions. The first is that women are in all the essential features identical with men and so have just as much right to ordination as men have. The second is that women are so different from men that an exclusively male priesthood cannot be fully representative of humanity. The third is that men have certain female characteristics and women have certain male ones, so that there is really only a difference of degree between the two; this is sometimes accompanied by the assertion that there is a maternal component in the fatherhood of God. The third argument has been advanced a good deal in recent years, but it would seem to lead to the opposite conclusion than that intended. For if it is true that the essential features of each sex are to be found in the other, then a male priest will be able to manifest in his pastoral relationships not only the male features but the female as well. The truth seems to be that there are many characteristics that are common to both sexes simply because they are both human, and many other characteristics that are proper only to one; but if we start by saying that female characteristics are to be found in men and male characteristics in women, we shall probably end up in a state of verbal confusion in which we shall find it difficult to maintain the distinction between male and female characteristics at all. It will be well to turn now to considerations of a more definitely theological kind.

THEOLOGICAL CONSIDERATIONS

As we have already seen, the Lambeth Conference of 1968 "affirm[ed] its opinion that the theological arguments as at present presented for and against the ordination of women to the priesthood are inconclusive" (Resolution 34). One might have thought that, if the arguments were as evenly balanced as that, there was, to say the least, insufficient justification for rejecting the agelong tradition of the Church; there would seem to he at least a prima facie case against making any drastic change. This was not, however, the Conference's conclusion. It is pertinent to ask, though there is little prospect of finding an answer, what the Conference supposed a conclusive theological argument would be. In common with most argumentation outside the purely abstract realm, theological arguments very rarely take the form of simple Aristotelian syllogisms. In the present case we have a consistent tradition of the Church going back to the very earliest times, and certain truths of faith which are closely coherent with that tradition and throw considerable light upon it. Though the Lambeth resolution did not mention these, the sub-committee did, though once again it combined verbal reverence with practical dismissal:

> The element of sexuality in the Godhead and its implication for the sex of the priesthood are complex and debatable matters. We acknowledge God as father and we worship the incarnate Lord as man. No theologian

has ever understood this to mean that God is male. There is great significance in the ancient imagery of the bishop or priest as father to his family or as representing Christ the bridegroom to the Church his bride. This is an image of unquestionable value, a profound pointer to the truth. But the truth to which it points has been expressed with equal power by St. Paul in referring to his own relation to the Galatian church as that of a mother again in travail with her children.

And the sub-commission asks the question, obviously expecting the answer No: "In view of the above considerations, are we to conclude that it nevertheless inheres in the very nature of the Gospel that women are intrinsically incapable of receiving ordination to the priesthood?"

"Great significance", "of unquestionable value", "profound pointer to the truth" – these are strong phrases indeed. They are nevertheless followed by the assertion, for which no further support is advanced than one sentence from St. Paul, the metaphorical sense of which is obvious, that in all relevant respects fatherhood and motherhood are identical. Once more we see doctrinal considerations treated as Plato in the *Republic* wished to treat the poet: "we shall do obeisance to him as to a sacred, wonderful and agreeable person, . . . and we shall anoint him with myrrh and crown him with a wreath of sacred wool and send him off to another city", for "we shall say that we have no such man in our city". I should like at this point to draw attention to a paper entitled "Priestesses in the Church?" by the late C. S. Lewis, which is included in the posthumously published volume *Undeceptions.*
Lewis begins by admitting that at first sight all the rationality

is on the side of the innovators. "We are short of priests. We have discovered in one profession after another that women can do very well all sorts of things which were once supposed to be in the power of men alone . . . . And against this flood of common sense, the opposers (many of them women) can produce at first nothing but an inarticulate distaste, a sense of discomfort which they themselves find it hard to analyse." However, "that this reaction does not spring from any contempt for women", Lewis significantly goes on to point out,

> is, I think, plain from history. The Middle Ages carried their veneration for one Woman to a point at which the charge could plausibly be made that the Blessed Virgin became in their eyes almost "a fourth Person of the Trinity". But never, so far as I know, in all those ages was anything remotely resembling a sacerdotal office attributed to her. All salvation depends on the decision which she made in the words *Ecce ancilla*; she is united in nine months' inconceivable intimacy with the eternal Word; she stands at the foot of the cross. But she is absent both from the Last Supper and from the descent of the Spirit at Pentecost. Such is the record of Scripture. Nor can you daff it aside by saying that local and temporary conditions condemned women to silence and private life. There were female preachers. One man had four daughters who all "prophesied", i.e., preached. There were prophetesses even in Old Testament times. Prophetesses, not priestesses.

"At this point", Lewis continues, "the common sensible reformer is apt to ask why, if women can preach, they cannot do all the rest of a priest's work. This question deepens the discomfort of my side." But "the more they speak (and speak truly) about the competence of women in administration, their tact and sympathy as advisers, their national [sic, qu. natural?] talent for visiting, the more we feel that the central thing is being forgotten." That thing is priesthood.

> Sometimes the priest turns his back on us and faces the East – he speaks to God for us: sometimes he faces us and speaks to us for God. We have no objection to a woman doing the first: the whole difficulty is about the second. But why? Why should a woman not in this sense represent God? Certainly not because she is necessarily, or even probably, less holy or less charitable or stupider than a man .... The sense in which she cannot represent God will perhaps be plainer if we look at the thing the other way round.
>
> Suppose the reformer stops saying that a good woman may be like God and begins by saying that God is like a good woman. Suppose he says that we might just as well pray to "Our Mother which art in heaven" as to "Our Father". Suppose he suggests that the Incarnation might just as well have taken a female as a male form, and the Second Person of the Trinity be as well called the Daughter as the Son. Suppose, finally, that the mystical marriage were reversed, that the Church were the Bridegroom and Christ the Bride. All this, as it seems to me, is involved in the claim that a woman can represent God as a priest does.

"Now it is surely the case", Lewis concludes, "that if all these supposals were ever carried into effect we should be embarked on a different religion. Goddesses have, of course, been worshipped: many religions have had priestesses. But they are religions quite different in character from Christianity."

There is only one place in which I would question Lewis's argument, but to strengthen rather than to weaken it. I am not sure that the priest speaks only to man from God and not also to God from man. It might, however, be replied that speaking to God from man, while it is a priestly function, is proper to the whole Church as the priestly body of Christ the great High Priest, even if its public and liturgical expression must be made through the ordained minister. Whatever may be true about this, the speaking to man of the reconciling word of God is an inherently personal and ministerial act. All Christian priesthood is the priesthood of Christ, whether exercised directly in his earthly life or mediately through his ordained ministers; and ministerial priesthood, as Moberley made clear in his great work bearing that name, is an essentially personal activity.

No doubt God in his omnipotence might have redeemed us by a sheer exercise of his infinite power and, so to speak, have *wrenched* us back into the shape which he wishes us to have. Nevertheless, God is personal – three Persons, united in one divine life – and we are persons; and he deals with us in accordance with his nature and ours. So the Second Person of the Holy Trinity, God the Son, took our human nature, so that he might live among us, a Person among persons, living, as one of us, that personal life of obedience and love to God the Father which culminated in a perfect human death and led through that death to a transformed and glorified, but still human and personal, life; teaching, healing, forgiving, consoling, strengthening those who came into contact with him, and always as a Person dealing with persons. God made man, the Son of God living a human life as a Person, living among persons and ministering to them as persons, this is the method that God chose to redeem the world; and the price of that method is shown by the Cross.

And when, after his Ascension, the Redeemer was no longer to be seen, heard and handled by our physical senses, he had already made provision that the ministry which he had exercised as a Person to persons should continue to be exercised by him *through* persons to persons. So he called and trained and commissioned and equipped twelve men whom he named *apostles* – persons sent – not just to be persons who would act instead of him but persons through whom he himself would act. So the sacramental and pastoral ministry of the Church through the ages, just because it is the ministry of the Person Jesus to persons for whom he gave his life, is exercised through persons, and through persons who are not just his representatives, not even just his agents, but the very organs through whom he himself acts. If there is this essential identity between the ministry which Jesus exercised in his earthly life and that which he now exercises in his Church, it is, to say the least, highly congruous that the manhood through which he acts should be male as he is male, whatever may be metaphysically possible to the sheer *potentia absoluta* of infinite Deity. But now to return to C. S. Lewis, after this lengthy but not irrelevant digression.

To the assertion that, if the masculine terms of religion, Father, Son and Bridegroom, were changed into the feminine terms, Mother, Daughter and Bride, we should have a different religion Lewis imagines "common sense" objecting "Why not? Since God is in fact not a biological being and has no sex, what can it matter whether we say *He* or *She*, *Father* or *Mother, Son* or *Daughter?*" Lewis's reply to this is that the Christian religion is in fact based on what God has said and done:

> Christians think that God Himself has taught us how to speak of Him. To say that it does not matter is to say either that all the masculine imagery is not inspired, is merely human in origin, or else that, though inspired, it is quite arbitrary and unessential. And this is surely intolerable: or, if tolerable, it is an argument not in favour of Christian priestesses but against Christianity. It is also surely based on a shallow view of imagery . . . a child who had been taught to pray to a Mother in Heaven would have a religious life radically different from that of a Christian child.

Thus, Lewis continues, "the innovators are really implying that sex is something superficial, irrelevant to the spiritual life. To say that men and women are equally eligible for a certain profession is to say that for the purposes of that profession their sex is irrelevant." To raise questions about the "equality" of the sexes is really pointless. "Unless 'equal' means 'interchangeable', equality makes nothing for the priesthood of women. . . . One of the ends for which sex was created was to symbolise to us the hidden things of God. One of the functions of human marriage is to express the nature of the union between Christ and the Church. We have no authority to take the living and sensitive figures which God has painted in the canvas of our nature and shift them about as if they were mere geometrical figures."

Lewis's discussion is all the more impressive coming as it does from a writer who was very little concerned with bloodless abstractions and was highly sensitive to the mysteries and depths of human nature as God has created and redeemed it.

And to him there was something superficial and undiscriminating in the concept of humanity, even on the natural level, that lay behind demands for the ordination of women to the priesthood. "With the Church" he wrote, "we are farther in: for we are dealing with male and female not merely as facts of nature but as the live and awful shadows of realities utterly beyond our control and largely beyond our direct knowledge. Or rather, we are not dealing with them but (as we shall soon learn if we meddle) they are dealing with us."

A VOICE FROM PROTESTANTISM

Very similar in some respects to Lewis's discussion is a very remarkable paper by the Calvinist theological Professor Jean-Jacques von Allmen of Neûchatel.[1] In view of my earlier stress upon the fact that we are concerned with the Catholic priesthood and not with various concepts of the Protestant ministry it will be well to make two points. First, von Allmen is a very high-church Protestant indeed, as anyone who has read his great book *Worship* will have discovered; there is no trace in him of Tillich's view that a minister differs from a layman only by his training. On the contrary, "the pastoral ministry is that grace, which the Lord has willed for the Church and instituted in the Church, by which one of the faithful, following on the Apostles, is called to act in the name of Christ the prophet, Christ the priest (*sacrificateur*) and Christ the King.... It is by the power of the Holy Spirit,

---

[1] "Is the Ordination of Women to the Pastoral Ministry justifiable?", *Verbum Caro*, XVII (1963), No. 65. The paper was first delivered to the Commission on Pastoral Ministry of the Reformed Church of France on 4th February, 1963. I quote from an English translation by the Rev. Herbert Moore, which exists in duplicated form.

invoked upon him at his ordination, that he is justified in exercising this ministry in the Church, and that he presumes to exercise it with confidence." Secondly, Calvinism has, of all forms of Protestantism, when it is true to its origins and traditions, the strongest sense of the Church as an organic and structured reality.

Von Allmen begins by stressing "the fact that in the Church everything is grace". "No one," he writes, "men no more than women, has the right to be a pastor. . . . You condemn yourself to never solving the problem when you say that it is unjust that women have not, as men have, the right to be a pastor; it is a grace which has not been purposed for them, because it would divert them from their being and their vocation, just as the grace of motherhood, for example, could not be given to a man." "Every ministry", he asserts, "is a grace. It does not depend then in the first place on the Church, but on the Lord of the Church; and if he has willed that among the ministries that of the pastor is to be reserved for men, the Church consequently has not the right to oppose this will by disobeying."

Von Allmen has a refreshingly independent attitude to the contemporary climate of opinion: "It could not be a question of progressive adaptation or reactionary obstinacy, for we are not called upon to comply with the present age, either in respect of what impels it forward or what restrains it; it is simply a question of obedience or disobedience, of faithfulness or unfaithfulness." It becomes clear later that this does not mean that God acts arbitrarily, without respect for the nature which he has given to mankind. Three major sets of arguments are given against the ordination of women to the pastoral ministry; the first is described as ecclesiological, the second as both anthropological and eschatological, and the third as ecumenical.

The ecclesiological argument replies to the assertion that, since women are admitted to faculties of theology and follow the same courses, offer the same work and pass the same examinations as men, they must be given the chance to practise the same profession. This assertion, von Allmen comments, assumes that "the pastoral ministry is not so much an institution of the Lord as an internal measure of ecclesiastical efficiency. . . The ministers are, then, kinds of ecclesiastical officials – ministers of the Church rather than ministers of Christ in the Church – responsible for doing what would be in short the task of the whole body of the faithful, but which cannot be demanded of them all, because it is not possible to disturb them all from their commitments involving family life or social, economic, political or cultural activities. . . . The Church then trains, enlists and supports 'theologians', who are a kind of full-time laity." (Von Allmen protests in passing against the assumption by Roman Catholics that such a view of the ministry is held by all Protestants.) "In fact," he adds, "if the pastoral ministry is only a full-time occupation for specialised laypeople, ordination, in the way that we traditionally practise it, is nonsense, indeed it is a contradiction and an error. For if the pastoral ministry is only that, baptism is sufficient for the valid exercise of it." The ministry would then be merely of the *bene esse* of the Church, not of its *esse*.

Behind this view von Allmen sees the influence of the Enlightenment, the *Aufklärung*:

> With complete disregard for the biblical doctrine of baptism, people go on affirming that from now on there is no longer any difference between the sacred and

the profane; and under the shelter of this proposition, they attempt to exclude from the Church anyone who would recall this difference, and thus also the difference between the clergy and the laity.

He penetratingly adds, no doubt with those in mind who will fear the implication that the clergy are "sacred" while the laity are merely "profane":

> Theologically this difference has nothing to do with the difference between the sacred and the profane, because it concerns a distinction within the sacred; but historically it can appear to give rise to this difference, since the Enlightenment is a cultural movement manifesting itself in western Christendom which had only too great an inclination to "make sacred" the clergy and secularise the laity.

"It is", he adds, "a 'desecration', a secularisation of the pastoral ministry to cease receiving it as a grace . . . to reduce it to an occupation in the internal organisation."

Von Allmen detects two other causes for the prevalence of this inadequate view of the ministry. The first is a wrong interpretation of the royal priesthood (sacrificature) of the people of God, an interpretation which arose at the time of the Reformation as a reaction against the extreme sacerdotalism of the Middle Ages; it has, he says, been more common among Lutherans than among Calvinists, and he gets in a sly dig at some modern Roman Catholic theologians for their "Lutheran approach". The second cause is the view that there is only one essential ministry in the Church, that of the Apostles and that, since the Apostles are no longer with us, it cannot be exercised by persons at all but only by the written testimony of the Apostles which is contained in the New Testament. His judgment on this point deserves to be quoted at length:

> I do not see, either in the New Testament, or among those who were the first to read it (the Fathers of the primitive Church), or among those who re-discovered it (the Reformers), the theory which would reduce the apostolic succession to the canonisation of apostolic writings; neither in the New Testament, nor in the Fathers, nor in the Reformers, do I find the assertion that the post-apostolic ministries, the ministries in the apostolic succession, do not belong to the Lord's institution, but to human invention; neither in the New Testament nor in the early Fathers, nor even in the Reformers, do I find the idea of a fundamental change in the Church just exactly at the death of the apostles, as if what came afterwards had no longer any actual relevance, had no longer any continuity, any genuine history, as if the Church did not have to continue, to last, without interruption, until the Parousia, and as if the pastoral ministry, the ministry in the apostolic succession, willed and instituted by Christ, was not precisely one of the graces by which he accompanies his people from one generation to another until his return. . . . And it is perhaps in this that the question of the ordination of women to the pastoral ministry is a most beneficial question: it will compel us to take up a position on the doctrine which among all of them makes us most uncomfortable, the doctrine of apostolic succession.

"But," von Allmen continues, "it will be said . . . can one not maintain in all its truth the doctrine, at once biblical, catholic and reformed, of the pastoral ministry while at the same time ordaining women to it, since henceforth in Christ 'there is neither male nor female'?" And this, he says, brings us to his second reason, which is both anthropological and eschatological.

Willingly accepting the text just quoted from Galatians iii, 28, he parallels it with three other Pauline texts: Romans x, 12, I Corinthians xii, 13 and Colossians iii, 11, but he remarks that all these are concerned with baptism, and he adduces six reasons why they cannot be extended to include the pastoral ministry. These merit consideration at length but I can only briefly summarise them here:

(1) It is untrue that St. Paul and the primitive Church shared the anti-feminist prejudices of their time. In many matters they showed themselves far more ready to challenge contemporary prejudices than are the Christians who criticise them today.

(2) The renewal which the Gospel brings to men and women alike does not invent, it restores: it recovers and revives what was "in the beginning". The New Testament and Pauline doctrine about women is based not on the Fall but on Creation. "The Gospel, in other words, does not save *from Creation*, it saves *Creation*; it does not rescue from the world willed by God, it rescues the world willed by God. Redemption does not contradict Creation, it vindicates it." To deny that there is a radical difference between man and woman in the order of redemption is to fall into Marcionism or Montanism – the precise heresies which had women priests!
(3) The polarisation of human beings into male and female

"is not an accident but affects them in their very identity and in their deepest mystery". This is why sexual sins are seen as not outside but "against" the sinner's body. People are called to serve the Lord *in* their masculinity or femininity. Further, Jesus was raised as male (*aner*), not just as human (*anthropos*), II Corinthians xi, 2.

(4) St. Paul's comparison of the nuptial union with the relation between Christ and the Church in Ephesians v is far too deeply theological for it to be possible to interchange Christ and the Church without falsifying and upsetting salvation. If the sexes were interchangeable St. Paul's argument of the "great mystery" would become artificial and shallow.

(5) Without encouraging odious male pretensions and arrogance, there is a "gradation" in mediation: "The head of every man is Christ, and the head of the woman is the man, and the head of Christ is God" (I Corinthians xi, 3). "God reaches men by Christ, and Christ reaches women by men. Which undoubtedly implies the converse also; just as men reach God by Christ, so women reach Christ by men." "It is no departure from this Pauline framework to say therefore that the work of God is transmitted through the mediation of Christ and, now that Christ has ascended into glory, through the derived and ministerial mediation of those whom he has charged to dispense the mysteries of God. Stated without safeguards and without qualifications, this means that between the Ascension and the Parousia, the mediator of grace among men is man rather than woman." Von Allmen expounds this notion at length:

> Expressing it in the terminology of Melanchthon, one can say that in the couple man represents the sacramental element, whereas woman represents the sacrificial element. But the sacramental element (he extends grace)

is not more than the sacrificial element (she gives back grace), since these two elements are both indispensable for the work of salvation to be achieved.

Von Allmen is emphatic that "this does not in any way disqualify woman, but assigns to her her specific place". And he makes some very suggestive final remarks:

> I do not think, however, that what we are unskilfully attempting to unravel here prevents Christian woman from also becoming the mediatrix of grace. But it means that if woman assumes this place, it is either when God temporarily dispenses with man (as in the virginal conception of Jesus), or else when man withdraws from his function of principal mediator of grace, as in the case of mixed marriages in which the husband is an unbeliever and the wife consequently becomes the justifying and sanctifying element (see I Corinthians vii, 14-16). . . .
>
> Woman could only accept and assume this place in the absence of any man or if men withdrew; then, perhaps and very exceptionally, it could be temporarily a course made tolerable by necessity. But so long as there are men in the Church, it would mean inflicting upon women a usurpation and on men a deprivation, by compelling women to forswear themselves in order to become ministers of the Word, the sacraments and discipline. For, even if they are holders of a Licence in Theology, what *is* a Licence in Theology in comparison with God's creation?

(6) "The New Testament, in spite of the chance of total renewal

which it provides for women as well as for men, never testifies that a woman could be, in a public and authorised way, representative of Christ." Although there were many women who could personally fulfil the requisite conditions, Christ gave all his ministerial commissions to men, and the Church never even considered a woman as a possible successor to Judas. "This is certainly not out of disdain, or because of masculine obstinacy, but through obedience." The events of Easter morning are normative:

> It was to women that Jesus appeared first in the record of Matthew, Mark and John. They were women who were the first witnesses of the empty tomb in the record of Luke. This is fresh proof of the importance which women acquired with the Gospel and by it. But to these first witnesses of . . . what is the heart and essence of the Gospel, Jesus does not say: Go and proclaim it to the world. He gives them the command to go and tell it to the Eleven. If Jesus had wished to invest them in the Church with the apostolic ministry of the Word, the sacraments and discipline, he would have charged them to go and proclaim to the world what they had seen and heard.

Lastly, von Allmen turns to ecumenical arguments. Stressing the uniformity of the Church's tradition against the ordination of women, he points out that the practice appears only in the nineteenth century and in circles in which the ministry itself is seen only as of the *bene esse* of the Church. "The Churches scandalised by such a measure understand . . . that by adopting the practice of ordaining women to the pastoral ministry, they would be doing much more than taking an internal administrative decision; they would be taking a fundamental and theological decision, which could not but have repercussions at once on the doctrine of the Church and the Ministry and on anthropology." And, remarking that the ecumenical problem presented by the ministry is already sufficiently complicated, von Allmen concludes that "a Church which refused to allow itself to be influenced by this argument would be lacking in love and in hope and, under the safe pretext of obedience, would be making a display of pride, of insensitiveness and even of sectarian spirit."

This concludes von Allmen's minute and comprehensive discussion of the ordination of women to the pastoral ministry. In a much shorter appended section of his paper he discusses, with approval and enthusiasm, the development of the female ministry of the diaconate. I shall not attempt to summarise it here, partly for reasons of space and also because the details of his exposition are more relevant to the conditions of a continental Calvinist Church than to those of the Churches of the Anglican Communion. It does, however, make it plain that he is not motivated by any anti-feminist bias. Looking back on his paper as a whole I find it both refreshing and profound. In contrast with most of the discussions to which we have become accustomed in this country, his argument has several very impressive features.

The first is his determination to raise the whole question above the sub-Christian level of rights, privileges and demands, and to see it as primarily concerned with simple obedience to the decisions and commands of God.

The second is his conviction that those decisions and

commands are not purely arbitrary but are coherent with human nature as God has created it.

The third is his recognition that the polarity of human nature as male and female is not a superficial or accidental differentiation, primarily concerned with the propagation of the species, but penetrates human nature to its most profound recesses.

The fourth is his insight that this polarity on the level of nature and creation has its analogue, and indeed its fulfilment, on the level of grace and redemption; mankind is bisexual by nature and bisexual too by grace.

The fifth is his detailed and exhaustive attention to the texts of the New Testament; unlike the Lambeth sub-committee, he is not content simply to throw together casually a couple of texts and then discard one of them.

Finally he provides an impressive example of the fact that opposition to the ordination of women to the priesthood is not the outcome of a crudely sacerdotal clericalism; indeed a secondary, but by no means unimportant result of his discussion, is a suggestion that a traditionally Calvinistic view of the ministry (as distinct from views characteristic of liberal Protestantism) may be much closer to that of a balanced and renewed Catholicism than one might have expected. In the most vigorous (which does not mean the most anarchistic) Catholic circles today there has appeared a recovery of the pastoral aspect of the priesthood which does not carry with it any derogation from the sacramental and kerygmatic aspects; this is at least similar to von Allmen's stress upon the minister's exercise of Christ's threefold office as prophet, priest and King. Here as in many other matters it has, I think, become clear that the real dividing line today is not between Catholicism and Protestantism in their authentic forms, but between those who believe in the fundamentally revealed and given character of the Christian religion and those who find their norms in the outlooks and assumptions of contemporary secularised culture and are concerned to assimilate the beliefs and institutions of Christianity to it.

CONCLUSION

It will I hope, be clear from the foregoing discussion that the extension of the ordained priesthood to women is by no means the natural and indeed inevitable development that many people today assume it to be, and that the case against it rests not upon masculine triumphalism and unreflective conservatism but upon serious theological and biblical principles. In bringing the discussion to a close I will make only two final remarks.

(1) The present epoch is one of animated and wide-ranging reconsideration of dogmatic and theological matters, and of these the nature of the Church and its ministry are not the least important. Their resolution will not be achieved overnight. It is conceivable, as a matter of pure logic, that the upshot will be a universal recognition that the priesthood is open to women as to men and that the arguments for the contrary position, such as those which have been expounded above, will have received satisfactory refutation and will be seen to be baseless. This is in my opinion unlikely and it is not in any case to be assumed in advance. In a period of theological

turbulence it is not legitimate, as many appear to think, that practical effect should be given to any revolutionary proposal that may suggest itself. On the contrary such a proposal needs the most searching examination; otherwise the Church may be found to have committed itself to an irreversible course of action that future generations will condemn as reflecting the ephemeral and unsubstantial prejudices of the latter part of the twentieth century. Those who dismiss the Church's past practice as socially conditioned and obsolete should seriously ask themselves whether their own proposals may not fall under the same condemnation. Sociology is a game at which more than one can play!

(2) Even if we leave theological considerations aside, it may well be questioned whether the contemporary world is capable of providing the Church with those guidelines for *aggiornamento* which it needs at the present day. Far from presenting the appearance of a social order which has discovered how to control and direct the tremendous forces which science and technology have released, it bears all the marks of a situation which has got thoroughly out of hand. The mere mention of such phrases as nuclear war, population explosion and environmental pollution is sufficient indication that the dominant influences in the world today have not yet discovered how to direct the world's own affairs, let alone those of the Church. I am not advocating that, in order to escape contamination by the perverse and ephemeral assumptions of the present day, the Church should cling on to the perverse and outmoded assumptions of the past. What I am advocating is that the Church should be loyal, both in ordering her own life and in presenting the Gospel to the contemporary world, to the revelation which she has received from God in Christ. And with regard to the special question with which we have here

been concerned, it would be naive in the extreme to suppose that the culture in which we live has been so successful in understanding the nature of sex and applying that understanding in practice as to be capable of providing the Church with principles for deciding such a matter as that of the ordination of women. On the contrary, the sexual chaos of the modern world would seem itself to show the need of such guidance as only the Christian revelation can give. No doubt it is true that in matters of sex the Church has picked up in the course of her history attitudes and assumptions that cannot be justified by Christian principles. It is all the more necessary that, having learnt the lesson, she shall explore those principles more thoroughly and not capitulate to the attitudes and assumptions of her present environment. And of no aspect of the matter is this more true than of the relation of sex to the priesthood.

PRIESTESSES IN THE CHURCH?

C.S. Lewis

1948

"I should like Balls infinitely better," said Caroline Bingley, "if they were carried on in a different manner ... It would surely be much more rational if conversation instead of dancing made the order of the day."

"Much more rational, I dare say," replied her brother, "but it would not be near so much like a Ball."

We are told that the lady was silenced: yet it could be maintained that Jane Austen has not allowed Bingley to put forward the full strength of his position. He ought to have replied with a distinguo. In one, sense conversation is more rational for conversation may exercise the reason alone, dancing does not. But there is nothing irrational in exercising other powers than our reason. On certain occasions and for certain purposes the real irrationality is with those who will not do so. The man who would try to break a horse or write a poem or beget a child by pure syllogizing would be an irrational man; though at the same time syllogizing is in itself a more rational activity than the activities demanded by these achievements. It is rational not to reason, or not to limit oneself to reason, in the wrong place; and the more rational a man is the better he knows this.

These remarks are not intended as a contribution to the criticism of Pride and Prejudice. They came into my head when I heard that the Church of England was being advised to declare women capable of Priests' Orders. I am, indeed, informed that such a proposal is very unlikely to be seriously considered by the authorities. To take such a revolutionary step at the present moment, to cut ourselves off from the Christian past and to widen the divisions between ourselves and other Churches by establishing an order of priestesses in our midst, would be an almost wanton degree of imprudence. And the Church of England herself would be torn in shreds by the operation. My concern with the proposal is of a more theoretical kind. The question involves something even deeper than a revolution in order.

[margin note: *Didn't happen.*] [bracket around "And the Church of England herself would be torn in shreds by the operation."]

I have every respect for those who wish women to be priestesses. I think they are sincere and pious and sensible people. Indeed, in a way they are too sensible. That is where my dissent from them resembles Bingley's dissent from his sister. I am tempted to say that the proposed arrangement would make us much more rational "but not near so much like a Church".

For at first sight all the rationality (in Caroline Bingley's sense) is on the side of the innovators. We are short of priests. We have discovered in one profession after another that women can do very well all sorts of things which were once supposed to be in the power of men alone. No one among those who dislike the proposal is maintaining that women are less capable than men of piety, zeal, learning and whatever else seems necessary for the pastoral office. What, then, except prejudice begotten by tradition, forbids us to draw on the huge reserves which could pour into the priesthood if women were here, as in so many other professions, put on the same footing as men? And against this flood of common sense, the opposers (many of them women) can produce at first nothing but an inarticulate distaste, a sense of discomfort which they themselves find it hard to analyse.

That this reaction does not spring from any contempt for women is, I think, plain from history. The Middle Ages carried their reverence for one Woman to a point at which the charge could be plausibly made that the Blessed Virgin became in their eyes almost "a fourth Person of the Trinity". But never, so far as I know, in all those ages was anything remotely resembling a sacerdotal office attributed to her. All salvation depends on the decision which she made in the words Ecce ancilla; she is united in nine months" inconceivable intimacy with the eternal Word; she stands at the foot of the cross." But she is absent both from the Last Supper and from the descent of the Spirit at Pentecost. Such is the record of Scripture. Nor can you daff it aside by saying that local and temporary conditions condemned women to silence and private life. There were female preachers. One man had four daughters who all "prophesied", i.e. preached. There were prophetesses even in Old Testament times. Prophetesses, not priestesses.

At this point the common sensible reformer is apt to ask why, if women can preach, they cannot do all the rest of a priest's work. This question deepens the discomfort of my side. We begin to feel that what really divides us from our opponents is a difference between the meaning which they and we give to the word "priest". The more they speak (and speak truly) about the competence of women in administration, their tact and sympathy as advisers, their national talent for "visiting", the more we feel that the central thing is

[margin note: I don't think that means respect for women only as mother, as women broadly.]

45

More work needs doing to argue this point.

being forgotten. To us a priest is primarily a representative, a double representative, who represents us to God and God to us. Our very eyes teach us this in church. Sometimes the priest turns his back on us and faces the East - he speaks to God for us: sometimes he faces us and speaks to us for God. We have no objection to a woman doing the first: the whole difficulty is about the second. But why? Why should a woman not in this sense represent God? Certainly not because she is necessarily, or even probably, less holy or less charitable or stupider than a man. In that sense she may be as "God-like" as a man; and a given women much more so than a given man. The sense in which she cannot represent God will perhaps be plainer if we look at the thing the other way round.

This has happened.

Suppose the reformer stops saying that a good woman may be like God and begins saying that God is like a good woman. Suppose he says that we might just as well pray to "Our Mother which art in heaven" as to "Our Father". Suppose he suggests that the Incarnation might just as well have taken a female as a male form, and the Second Person of the Trinity be as well called the Daughter as the Son. Suppose, finally, that the mystical marriage were reversed, that the Church were the Bridegroom and Christ the Bride. All this, as it seems to me, is involved in the claim that a woman can represent God as a priest does.

Now it is surely the case that if all these supposals were ever carried into effect we should be embarked on a different religion. Goddesses have, of course, been worshipped: many religions have had priestesses. But they are religions quite different in character from Christianity. Common sense, disregarding the discomfort, or even the horror, which the idea of turning all our theological language into the feminine

[Handwritten annotation at top: Good argument against 'gender = biology.']

gender arouses in most Christians, will ask "Why not? Since God is in fact not a biological being and has no sex, what can it matter whether we say He or She, Father or Mother, Son or Daughter?"

But Christians think that God Himself has taught us how to speak of Him. To say that it does not matter is to say either that all the masculine imagery is not inspired, is merely human in origin, or else that, though inspired, it is quite arbitrary and unessential. And this is surely intolerable: or, if tolerable, it is an argument not in favour of Christian priestesses but against Christianity. It is also surely based on a shallow view of imagery. Without drawing upon religion, we know from our poetical experience that image and apprehension cleave closer together than common sense is here prepared to admit; that a child who has been taught to pray to a Mother in Heaven would have a religious life radically different from that of a Christian child. And as image and apprehension are in an organic unity, so, for a Christian, are human body and human soul.

The innovators are really implying that sex is something superficial, irrelevant to the spiritual life. To say that men and women are equally eligible for a certain profession is to say that for the purposes of that profession their sex is irrelevant. We are, within that context, treating both as neuters.

As the State grows more like a hive or an ant-hill it needs an increasing number of workers who can be treated as neuters. This may be inevitable for our secular life. But in our Christian life we must return to reality. There we are not homogeneous units, but different and complementary organs of a mystical body. Lady Nunburnholme has claimed that the equality of men and women is a Christian principle. I do not

[Handwritten annotation at bottom: I do think it feels like the only way to participate is through ministry.]

remember the text in scripture nor the Fathers, nor Hooker, nor the Prayer Book which asserts it; but that is not here my point. The point is that unless "equal" means "interchangeable", equality makes nothing for the priesthood of women. And the kind of equality which implies that the equals are interchangeable (like counters or identical machines) is, among humans, a legal fiction. It may be a useful legal fiction. But in church we turn our back on fictions. One of the ends for which sex was created was to symbolize to us the hidden things of God. One of the functions of human marriage is to express the nature of the union between Christ and the Church. We have no authority to take the living and semitive figures which God has painted on the canvas of our nature and shift them about as if they were mere geometrical figures.

This is what common sense will call "mystical". Exactly. The Church claims to be the bearer of a revelation. If that claim is false then we want not to make priestesses but to abolish priests. If it is true, then we should expect to find in the Church an element which unbelievers will call irrational and which believers will call supra-rational. There ought to be something in it opaque to our reason though not contrary to it - as the facts of sex and sense on the natural level are opaque. And that is the real issue. The Church of England can remain a church only if she retains this opaque element. If we abandon that, if we retain only what can be justified by standards of prudence and convenience at the bar of enlightened common sense, then we exchange revelation for that old wraith Natural Religion.

It is painful, being a man, to have to assert the privilege, or the burden, which Christianity lays upon my own sex. I am crushingly aware how inadequate most of us are, in our actual and historical individualities, to fill the place prepared for us. But it is an old saying in the army that you salute the uniform not the wearer. Only one wearing the masculine uniform can (provisionally, and till the Parousia) represent the Lord to the Church: for we are all, corporately and individually, feminine to Him. We men may often make very bad priests. That is because we are insufficiently masculine. It is no cure to call in those who are not masculine at all. A given man may make a very bad husband; you cannot mend matters by trying to reverse the roles. He may make a bad male partner in a dance. The cure for that is that men should more diligently attend dancing classes; not that the ballroom should henceforward ignore distinctions of sex and treat all dancers as neuter. That would, of course, be eminently sensible, civilized, and enlightened, but, once more, "not near so much like a Ball".

And this parallel between the Church and the Ball is not so fanciful as some would think. The Church ought to be more like a Ball than it is like a factory or a political party. Or, to speak more strictly, they are at the circumference and the Church at the Centre and the Ball comes in between. The factory and the political party are artificial creations - "a breath can make them as a breath has made". In them we are not dealing with human beings in their concrete entirety only with "hands" or voters. I am not of course using "artificial" in any derogatory sense. Such artifices are necessary: but because they are our artifices we are free to shuffle, scrap and experiment as we please. But the Ball exists to stylize something which is natural and which concerns human beings in their entirety-namely, courtship. We cannot shuffle or tamper so much. With the Church, we are farther in: for there we are dealing with male and female not merely as facts of nature but as the live and awful shadows of realities utterly beyond our control and largely beyond our direct knowledge. Or rather, we are not dealing with them but (as we shall soon learn if we meddle) they are dealing with us.

TEN OBJECTIONS TO WOMEN PRIESTS

A. Linsley

2019

As a woman who served as a priest in the Episcopal Church for 16 years, I have some experience of the nature of the priesthood. In 1982, with the encouragement of my parish clergy, friends and family, it seemed the right course for my life. Over the years, I began to question the rationale for women priests. I remember feeling that I was standing in another's shoes, not appropriately mine. I wanted to explain this to my bishop, but he clearly did not want to hear it.

Galatians 3:28 has been used to justify the innovation of women priests: "There is neither Jew nor Gentile, neither slave nor free, nor is there male and female, for you are all one in Christ Jesus." In the fourth century, St. Epiphanius remarked that the heretical Cataphyrgians (Montanists) employed Galatians 3:28 to elevate women as "bishops and priests and they say nothing makes a difference 'For in Christ Jesus there is neither male nor female.'" (*Panarion 49.2*)

Reading Galatians 3:28 in context, it is apparent that Paul is speaking of the unity of the body of Christ. He is not promoting gender equality as it is framed today. As the Supper was intended to unite the participants to the Head, Jesus Christ, the idea of a woman presiding at the Feast would have been unthinkable.

My doubts made the priestly ministry increasingly burdensome and problematic. As a heterosexual, Bible-believing, Anglican Traditionalist, I found no affirmation in the Episcopal Church as it moved toward a radical revision of the Gospel, setting aside the Apostolic Tradition for its social justice agenda.

Eventually, I renounced orders in the Episcopal Church and left that body. This initiated a decade of reflection on the role of women in the Church and the historic priesthood. During that time, I was in conversation with three former women priests who were seeking clarity also. One entered the Roman Catholic Church and the others entered the Orthodox Church of America. I explored both traditions, but I am thoroughly Anglican and have been for forty-three years.

I have written on the question of women priests, exploring it through Biblical studies, Church history, and cultural anthropology. As with many Anglicans, I believe that the Episcopal Church erred in 1976 when it departed from the all-male priesthood. On a single day the General Convention of the Episcopal Church overthrew catholic orders, rejected the teaching of the Fathers, and denied the authority of Holy Scripture.

Historically, the priesthood of the Church was restricted to a few chosen men, tested and carefully formed for the priestly office. In his treatise "On the Priesthood," St. John Chrysostom wrote, "When one is required to preside over the Church, and be entrusted with the care of so many souls, the whole female sex must retire before the magnitude of the task, and the majority of men also."

Not a single woman served in the office of priest until 1944, at which time Florence Li Tim-Oi was ordained by Ronald Hall, Bishop of Victoria, Hong Kong, in response to the crisis among Anglicans in Communist China. She later stepped down from serving as a priest.

The first woman "canonically" ordained to the priesthood in the United States was a lesbian who served as Integrity's first co-president. Other lesbians had been among the Philadelphia Eleven. In the United States, the ordination of women and homosexuals was so intertwined from the beginning that it is difficult to treat these as separate questions. Both have been framed as "equal rights" issues, revealing a profound misunderstanding of the priesthood. The priesthood is not a right, and it is not a reward to be bestowed upon those who will advance a body's agenda.

In this paper I address ten reasonable objections to women in the priesthood:

1. The Church is not a democratic body.
2. Women's ordination is linked to homosexual activism.
3. Women's ordination is rooted in Feminist thought.
4. Women priests perpetuate confusion about gender.
5. Women priests represent rejection of the authority Scripture and Tradition.

6. Women priests cause confusion about the Eucharist.
7. Women priests represent a denial of the Fathers' teaching.
8. Ordination of women to the priesthood undermines women's ministries.
9. The feminization of the clergy discourages men's participation in the church.
10. A female at the altar blurs the biblical distinction between life and death.

1. THE CHURCH IS NOT A DEMOCRACY

In 1994, Pope John Paul II spoke ex cathedra on female ordination, observing that the male priesthood had been "preserved by the constant and universal Tradition of the Church and clearly taught by the Magisterium in recent documents." He stated that the Church has "no authority to confer priestly ordination on women."

Synods may vote to conform "the constant and universal Tradition of the church" to the world's shifting values. That invariably results in the loss of spiritual heritage and places the body outside the catholic Faith, which is where the Episcopal Church is today.

No jurisdiction has authority to set aside the all-male priesthood. The Body of Christ does not concede to the unilateral action of the Episcopal Church. The Church is not a democratic body in which dogma, doctrine, and the received tradition are changed or set aside by a vote.

2. WOMEN'S ORDINATION IS LINKED TO HOMOSEXUAL ACTIVISM

Historically, a clear link exists between the push for women priests and homosexual activism. In 1974, the same year that

Louie Crew founded the homosexual activist organization Integrity, eleven women, including known lesbians, were ordained in Philadelphia.

In September 1975, more lesbians were ordained in Washington D.C. Here is the account in Louie Crew's words: "More 'irregular' ordinations of women took place... after our convention. In Washington at the time, on a missionary journey to our new chapters in the east, Jim Wickliff and I yielded to the counsel of friends who advised that our visibility at the ordination might put in jeopardy lesbians among all early ordinands."

In 1976 the General Convention of the Episcopal Church affirmed homosexual behavior when it passed the "we are children of God" resolution.

In 1977, Bishop Paul Moore (NY) ordained Ellen Marie Barrett, who had served as Integrity's first co-president.

Breaking catholic orders was necessary to opening the priesthood to partnered gay and lesbian persons.

3. WOMEN'S ORDINATION IS ROOTED IN FEMINIST THOUGHT.

Ideological Feminism is not about equal pay for equal work. It is not an ideology of love, forgiveness, reconciliation, and equality. It is a Marxist ideology that reframes the economic antagonism between classes as a struggle between men and women. As in Marxism, radical feminism seeks to shift control of institutions and society to women. As such, ideological Feminism must oppose biblical headship as an expression of the sovereignty of God Father and God Son.

Feminist arguments are usually baseless and often irrational. Susan Cornwall argues that women can be priests because Jesus was a woman. By this ridiculous assertion she hopes to confront "discrimination against women" which she believes "is based on the tradition of Jesus having chosen only male apostles."

In 2015, Canon Emma Percy of the Church of England said, "In the last two or three years we've seen a real resurgence and interest in feminism, and younger people are much more interested in how gender categories shouldn't be about stereotypes. We need to have a language about God that shows God can be expressed in lots of diverse terms."

Percy wants to speak of God Father and God Mother. Attacking a straw man argument, she said, "Using both male and female language would get rid of the notion that God is some kind of old man in the sky."

4. WOMEN PRIESTS PERPETUATE CONFUSION ABOUT GENDER.

Why draw the line at male and female language for God? On this slippery slope we may slide into casting God as transgendered or, like a crossdresser, being one gender but appearing as another. In a New York Times Opinion piece (Aug. 2016), Rabbi Mark Sameth makes a case for gender fluidity by citing examples in the Bible of male and female pronouns being exchanged or reversed. However, Sameth never claims that the God of the Hebrew Scriptures is transgender.

Jacques Derrida and others have noted that gender reversals in literature point to mystery. Derrida noted that in narratives when a gender reversal takes place, the other becomes the dominant voice. Normally, the dominant voice is that of the Male Principle/Presence, but when the reversal takes place, the Female Principle/Presence is in action. There are many examples of this in the Old Testament which explains why the Hebrew pronouns are sometimes ambiguous.

Genesis 3:15, the earliest Messianic reference in the Bible, is the most striking example of the mystery of gender reversal. The Hebrew says, "He will crush you a head and you will crush us a heel." The subject of the verb is the third person, masculine, singular (he) and the imperfect tense of the verb indicates action yet to be completed. The suffix –*khaf* identifies the object of the verb as second person, masculine, singular (you). This would be translated as "he will crush you" and the message is directed to the serpent.

In the Vulgate, St. Jerome gives "ipsa" as the nominative feminine singular of ipse though ipsa is sometimes the nominative neuter plural. Jerome's rendering of Genesis 3:15 reads: Inimicitias ponam inter te et mulierem, et semen tuum et semen illius: ipsa conteret caput tuum, et tu insidiaberis calcaneo eius. God says to the serpent, "I will put enmities between you and the woman, between your offspring and her offspring. She will crush your head, and you will lie in wait for her heel."

In his *Commentaria in Scripturam Sacram* the Jesuit priest Cornelius a Lapide (1567-1637) recognized the significance of gender reversal in the Hebrew Bible. He resolved the problem of the verb in the masculine (yashuph, conteret), citing the interplay of gender in Hebrew: the masculine being used in place of the feminine and vice-versa when there is some mystery, anomaly, or singularity. Lapide wrote, "frequent exchange of gender in Hebrew: the masculine being used in place of the feminine and vice-versa, especially when there is present some cause or mystery."

5. WOMEN PRIESTS REPRESENT REJECTION OF THE AUTHORITY OF SCRIPTURE AND TRADITION

The fact that the gender exchange involves only male and female indicates that the biblical view of humanity is binary, not transgender, not homosexual, and not a spectrum.

Though the interplay of male and female language in Scripture hints at the mystery of the Godhead, it does not pertain to God. In Christianity, God has self-revealed as Father of the Son, Jesus Christ. As Fr. Thomas Hopko recognized, "In his actions in and toward the world of his creation, the one God and Father reveals himself primarily and essentially in a 'masculine' way." (Women and the Priesthood, p 240.)

The Church's relationship to God is expressed in the language it uses in prayer and the language it uses in speaking about God. That is exactly why we preserve the biblical language for God Father and God Son. The language is not negotiable. "Whoever denies the Son does not have the Father; whoever confesses the Son has the Father as well." (1 John 2:23) This is the kerygma, as John makes clear: "And we have seen and testify that the Father has sent His Son to be the Savior of the world. If anyone confesses that Jesus is the Son of God, God abides in him, and he in God." (1 John 4:14-15)

The language of God Father and God Son is as essential to the Gospel as the dogmas of Jesus' two natures and the Trinity.

Those who applaud women priests acknowledge that women at the altar change the way we think about God. The Rev. Serene Jones, the first woman president of Union Theological Seminary, said exactly that: "When the people who are representing God, making God present, have female bodies, that inevitably changes the way you think about how God is."

This revisionist language represents a rejection of the Bible's authority. Setting aside the language of the Bible is preliminary to replacing holy men at the altar. Females and persons who identify as "other" claim presidency at the Eucharist. They change the traditional prayers according to their whims and dismiss the formularies of the catholic Faith. They invent narratives to work around Scripture and Tradition since they have dismissed the received Faith as sexist, patriarchal, and outdated.

6. WOMEN PRIESTS CAUSE CONFUSION ABOUT THE EUCHARIST.

When Anglicans contemplate reception of Christ's Body and Blood in the Eucharist, it is appropriate to see before them a masculine form. Likewise, in contemplation of the Annunciation and Incarnation we properly have before us an image/icon of Mary, not a masculine form. The narrative of gender equality at the altar changes the sign of His sacrifice, resurrection, and promise of immortality to the baptized. It reframes the Eucharist to avoid the reality of Jesus, the Male God. The product is sadly inferior, as it resembles pagan commemorative feasts.

7. WOMEN PRIESTS REPRESENT A DENIAL OF THE FATHERS' TEACHING.

The invented narrative also represents a denial of the authority of the Church Fathers who urge diligence in maintaining the received Tradition. Ignatius of Antioch adjures, "Be diligent, therefore, to use one eucharist, for there is one flesh of our Lord Jesus Christ, and one cup, for union with his blood; one altar, even as there is one bishop, together with the presbytery and the deacons who are my fellow-servants, to the end that whatever ye do, ye may do it according unto God. (Philadelphians 4.1)

Women priests are evidence of the Western church's love of innovation. Speaking against this tendency, St. Basil the Great wrote, "The dogmas of the Fathers are held in contempt, the Apostolic traditions are disdained, the churches are subject to the novelties of innovators" (Letter 90, To the Most Holy Brethren and Bishops Found in the West). The Great Schism of 1054, and the lesser fractures that produced a plethora of denominations, come from pride and innovation.

The Church Fathers have a clear consensus on the question of women and the priesthood. St. Epiphanius, in "Against Heresies" (79.304), wrote: "If women were ordained to be priests for God or to do anything canonical in the church, it should rather have been given to Mary. . . She was not even entrusted with baptizing. Although there is an order of deaconesses in the church, yet they are not appointed to function as priests, or for any administration of this kind, but so that provision may be made for the propriety of the female sex [at nude baptisms]. Whence comes the recent myth? Whence comes the pride of women or rather, the woman's insanity?"

In his treatise "On the Priesthood" (3.9) St. John Chrysostom wrote: "Divine law has excluded women from the sanctuary, but they try to thrust themselves into it."

St. Augustine, "On Heresies" (27) refers to the heretical Pepuzians mentioned by St. Epiphanius. "They give such principality to women that they even honor them with priesthood."

8. THE ORDINATION OF WOMEN TO THE PRIESTHOOD UNDERMINES WOMEN'S MINISTRIES.

The Episcopal Church's top-down corporate model of leadership has not encouraged lay women in local ministries. Instead, the Episcopal Church proudly elevates women to the episcopacy. In 2019, seven women were elected as diocesan or suffragan bishops. Women with leadership gifts are needed to organize and lead vital ministries in the parishes, in prisons, and to oversee outreach to the poor, elderly, and sick. They are not needed as priests and bishops, roles that isolate them from other women and from grass root ministries. The priesthood by its very nature is isolating. Women priests often feel doubly isolated from parishioners and from a church leadership that regards them as a social justice issue.

9. THE FEMINIZATION OF THE CLERGY DISCOURAGES MEN'S PARTICIPATION IN THE CHURCH.

In his 1999 book The Church Impotent: The Feminization of Christianity, Leon Podles looked at attendance trends in Roman Catholic and Protestant churches and noted that the more liberal Protestant churches saw a decrease in male attendance from 47% to 40-35% between 1952 and 1986.

The trend is evident in the Church of England. In 1994, thirty-two women were ordained as priests in the Church of England. A February 2014 report in The Guardian states that between 2002 and 2012, the number of female full-time clergy increased by 41%. During the same period, the number of full-time male clergy dropped from 7,920 to 6,017.

The 2018 report reveals that the number of female clergy in the Church of England continues to rise with more women than men preparing for ordained ministry for the second year running.

From 2017 to 2018, the proportion of senior posts such as dean or bishop occupied by women rose from 23% to 25%. The figures do not include the six new female bishops in 2018, bringing the total number of female bishops in the Church of England to 24.

The 1992 decision to ordain women to the priesthood in the Church of England has been followed by the stated objective of having a 50%-50% census. To accomplish this means pushing women forward and denying some men.

Perhaps of greater importance is the number of fathers who regularly attend worship. Studies have shown that fathers are the greatest influence on whether their children also attend church. Writing on the importance of fathers in church, Robbie Low said, "To minister to a fatherless society, these churches, in their unwisdom, have produced their own single-parent family parish model in the woman priest."

10. A FEMALE AT THE ALTAR BLURS THE BIBLICAL DISTINCTION BETWEEN LIFE AND DEATH.

Speaking from the perspective of Biblical Anthropology, the priesthood of the Church stands in continuity with the Hebrew priesthood that was known to Abraham and his ancestors. As the author of Hebrews attests, Jesus is the perfect embodiment of that ancient priestly office (Hebrews 7:17). The priest's office is unique, deeply rooted in archaic religion, and stands as an ensign of the hope for immortality.

Anthropological research indicates that the priesthood originated among people who observed the binary distinction of male and female blood work. The priesthood is about blood sacrifice and blood covering. Consider the context of blood work in traditional societies. Men do the blood work that involves taking life: combat, hunting, and animal sacrifice. Women do the blood work that involves giving life: the monthly blood flow, and blood from the birth process.

Women were never priests because women were not permitted in the place of blood work that involves death. Likewise, men were not allowed in the birthing hut. The gender roles reflect the distinction between life and death, a distinction that God warns the covenant people not to blur. "This day I call the heavens and the earth as witnesses against you that I have set before you life and death, blessings and curses. Now choose life, so that you and your children may live…" (Deuteronomy 30: 15-20). A woman at the altar represents confusion about the binary nature of blood work in the biblical context.

The blood work of Jesus, the Son of God, is unique. His work on the Cross is both condemnation to those who are perishing and life to those who are being saved (Romans 1:16; 1 Corinthians 1:18-21). The faithful priest is a man whose life is a testimony to the reality of the blood of Christ, the cup of salvation.

HOLY ORDERS AND *AUTHENTEIN*

B. Jefferies

2020

ON AUTHENTEIN IN 1 TIMOTHY 2:12

I would like to zoom in on what may be the central issue within the whole debate concerning women's ordination: the word *authentein* in 1 Timothy 2:12.

I hope all Anglicans would agree with the following Syllogism: *If* — (I am not here assuming the point) — if it were the case that *authentein* ultimately means simply having authority, and if the Ephesian situation into which 1 Timothy is addressed is not that unique but is comparable to the situation faced by the rest of the Church, in the late first century as well as the late twenty-first, then it would be the case that the prohibition on women teaching and having authority in 1 Timothy 2:12 would be an interpretive key for expounding the rest of Scripture in a non-repugnant key: The female prophesying in 1 Cor 11, the female co-laborers in Philippians 4:2-3, Prisca in Acts, etc. — are all to be understood more as "catechists" "small-group leaders" and "teachers" rather than "priests" and "preachers" in the way those words signify today, since "priest" and "preacher" are roles that fall under "teaching and having authority over men" in the Church today, which 1 Tim 2:12 forbids if the above conditions are indeed the case.

So to the lynch-pin I shall turn, seeking to establish these two premises, with the hopes that, given the above proposition, if I can make the case convincingly, the foundation — at the level of exegetical details — may perhaps begin to be laid for the resolution of "dual integrities" into integrity.

For this work, I do not profess to any novel scholarship, rather, it seems to me that much excellent scholarship remains sequestered in scholarly and denominational silos. If the relevant scholarship is brought together in one place, organized according to Anglican epistemological principles, I believe a clearer solution can be seen to help unfreeze the deadlock on the issue of Women's Ordination in the Anglican Church.

ON THE NON-UNIQUENESS OF EPHESUS

The first thing to be established is that 1 Timothy is not being written into a highly unusual situation. If it was highly unusual, then there is the possibility (*pace*, the letter still being canonical Scripture) that the prohibition on women teaching and exercising/usurping authority was a local pastoral consideration and not a directive for the church universal. It is worth noting that there is not a single prohibition in the entire New Testament that the Church has rejected, on the grounds of it being a "local matter". With positive injunctions it is a more complex story, but with prohibitions, to make an exception for 1 Timothy 2:12 is to make a hermeneutical move that is *sui generis*, I.e. shaky ground to be standing on.

Nevertheless, the contention has been made (and is often assumed) that Ephesus was a very unique setting in which women had exceptional authority and that this local cultural norm was infiltrating the otherwise decent relating between men and women in the Church. The Temple of Artemis (in Ephesus) which had female "clergy" is often pointed to as a signal indicator of Ephesian uniqueness.

But was it really unique? S.M. Baugh in *A Foreign World: Ephesus in the First Century* makes the case very convincingly that it was not. It startles me that this paper, contained in *Women in the Church* (Third Edition, Eds. Köstenberger and Schreiner, Crossway, 2016) is not cited more frequently, because the quantity of primary text data presented is nigh unarguable in its defense of Baugh's conclusion,

"Ephesus was in most ways a typical Hellenic society…Like other Greco-Roman city-states, its society was generally patriarchal." (p. 60)

This is over and against the modern feminist interpreters who might leave

"the impression that ancient Ephesus was some fanciful gynocracy." (p. 50)
While women in the ancient world were not universally the kitchen-maids of feminist folk-history, it was still the case that even in Ephesus men held positions of civic honor in

ratios approaching 100:1, that the temple of Artemis was not independent but still under the rule of the Roman government, etc.

Moreover, there were priestesses in many cults, throughout the Roman Empire, and religious devotion was as pluriform and variegated in Ephesus as in all other cities. In other words, there is very little to distinguish Ephesus from its wider religious milieu.

There is nothing in the Sitz im Leben of 1 Timothy that would suggest an extraordinary circumstance prompting extraordinary behavior in the Church as a matter of course.

I point readers to Baugh's excellent essay for further details supporting the case.

EPHESUS COMPARED TO THE PRESENT DAY

If feminist scholars cannot substantially distinguish Ephesus from its milieu, then a fall-back manoeuvre might be to lump it together with its milieu in its un-enlightened thinking about women and their roles, and then make the contrast with 21st century understandings of the same. However, this approach also falls flat when the actual details of life in a large Roman city in the mid first century are teased out, as they have been by Bruce Winter in his seminal *Roman Wives, Roman Widows* (Eerdmans, 2003).

What Winter demonstrates with ample archeological and primary source evidence throughout the entire book is that the first century saw the rise of the then-called "new woman".

That, in the face of great prosperity across the empire and the concomitant decadence, traditional gender roles were being challenged by influential women who started a movement of sorts (A sociologist might say because the traditional roles were no longer "needed" for economic stability). In Neronian Rome (the era of 1 Timothy), the "new women" were asserting themselves in unprecedented numbers as lawyers and political figures across the empire, and traditional mores of courting and sexuality were being flouted, along with the newly acquired titles of respect.

"The 'new' wife or widow in the late Roman Republic and early Empire was the one whose social life was reported to have been pursued at the expense of family responsibilities" and who engaged in "the new activities that certain women of means engaged in outside the family and in the wider society, both in business and in the public place." (Roman Wives, Roman Widows, 4-5) "These new women had an unsettling influence on the status quo" (Ibid., 38)

This is the world into which 1 Timothy was written. Does it sound familiar? It sounds a lot like the West since the 1960s. In other words, if Paul's words to Timothy were appropriate then, they are a fortiori appropriate now.

In other words, the letters to Timothy are universal, they are applicable to the whole church, across time and space, and are not merely products of Ephesian oddities.

Having established this, let us now turn to the crux of the matter, the greek word αὐθεντεῖν (*authentein*), the infinitive form of the verb authenteo, that occurs in 1 Tim 2:12.

The ESV renders 1 Tim 2:12 as "I do not permit a woman to teach or to exercise authority (*authentein*) over a man." Let's examine the validity of this translation.

OF AUTHENTEIN AND AUTHORITY

Scholars who believe the Bible does not prohibit women in ordained ministry believe that the word in this case should be translated more pejoratively, such as "usurp authority" or even "to domineer", and that St. Paul is only ordering them not to exercise this abuse of authority, not authority in itself. Fr. McCaulley alludes to this long-standing discussion when he writes,

"What is the difference between that word [αὐθεντεῖν] and the more common ἐξουσία?" [exousia, the word most used in the NT for 'authority']

In other words — implying that there is a difference, that the Bible doesn't forbid women exercising authority (exousia) only bad or ursuped authority (authentien).

Now, the majority consensus among Biblical scholars is that *authentein* is best rendered as simply "authority", witness NRSV (hardly a 'conservative' creation): "I permit no woman to teach or to have authority over a man."

But there has been a challenge to this interpretation, lately fueled by a disproportionately influential paper by James Hübner (also cited by Fr. McCaulley), that asserts the pejorative quality of *authentein* — that it is not a "neutral" word. (Cynthia Westfall's recent treatment is hopelessly obfuscated by her lengthy appeal to a particular linguistic theory, and I think this accounts for the popularity of the Hübner article).

Since *authentein* occurs nowhere else in the New Testament (a hapax legomenon), NT scholars appeal to the usage of the word in other previous or near-contemporary Greek writings.

The second edition of Women in the Church had a good essay on this question, but it was blown out of the water by the dissertation Al Wolters supplies in the third edition (which came out after Hübner's article).

Against the works of Westfall, Hübner and others, Wolters spends sixty pages turning over every linguistic stone in an effort to recover a strong probable sense of the meaning of the word *authentein*. His conclusion is definitive: it is a neutral word meaning simply 'authority', which I invite the reader to examine for themselves.

However, since both Hübner and Wolters possess more faculty than I do in analyzing the Greek, and I am therefore unable to personally arbitrate between their competing conclusions, It is worth pointing out that even if Hübner et al. are right (and I do not think they are), this doesn't accomplish their desired purpose of egalitarianizing 1 Tim 2:12, but just as easily makes the case for Paul's prohibition on women stronger, since it could very reasonably be synthesized that St. Paul sees women having authority in the church as ipso facto being an usurpation. If *authentein* is pejorative, it may be pejorative because the thing itself (women having authority over men) is looked down upon. This certainly seems to be the only explanation for why the translators of the KJV in 1611 would render it, "usurp authority", a fact not sufficiently reckoned with in Hübner's discussion.

Acknowledging this irony, it is still worth establishing that *authentein* is not pejorative in sense, and, to help us decided between the competing presentation of scholars (Wolters et al. versus Hübner et al.), as Anglican students of the Bible we can ask the question, "How was it understood by the Tradition of the Early Church?" In the terminology of biblical lexical studies, "what is the post-history of *authentein*?" How was the word later used by Church Fathers who read 1 Tim 2, most of whom were themselves native Greek speakers? We would expect the meaning of the word as it sits in 1 Tim 2:12 to have an effect on its usage in the later church, and, moreover, when missional circumstances prompted the translating of the New Testament books into other languages, the semantic footprint is sure to reveal itself.

For Anglicans who inhabit a church and an an ecclesiology that emphasizes organic continuity with the past, and for whom the Church Fathers (and Church Tradition generally) is a weighty factor in interpretation, this post-history would prima facie be of even greater weight than scholarly re-constructions of a words' meaning based on fragmentary pre-1st century textual evidence.

Wolters unearths the relevant details of the post-history of *authentein*, but writing as he does within a Reformed/Evangelical circle — where historical-grammatical criticism is de rigeur — he intentionally under-appreciates the gravity of the data (p.89), and further weakens the strength of the presentation by allocating usage into "columns" that are too subtle in their differentiation. Allow me to present it for the re-evaluation of an Anglican readership:

POST-HISTORY PART 1: THE FATHERS

Across nearly 100 uses of the verb authenteo, the Church Fathers almost exclusively use the word in a normal, non-pejorative sense.

The majority (51) of these usages have a connotation of "acting on one's own authority" (*Women in the Church*, p.97)

In many cases it is used to describe the way in which Jesus in his earthly ministry did only that which he saw his Father doing, such as St. John Chrysostom's comment on Jesus' prayer before the raising of Lazarus,

"Therefore, he [Jesus] who had raised countless dead men with a mere word, also added a prayer when he was calling Lazarus…'I said these things because of the crown standing around, in order that they might believe that you sent me.' And he neither does all things as one acting on his own authority (*authenton*)…nor does he do all things with prayer…as though he were weak and powerless." (Chrysostom's 16th Homily on Matthew)

The verb is also often used to describe the authority that God has (which could hardly be seen as pejorative!), such as Eusebius of Caesarea, who, commenting on the Trinitatian Baptismal formula writes,

"The Father being sovereign (*authentountos*) and bestowing grace, the Son administering this grace…etc."

Summing up his evaluation of patristic use of the word, Wolters concludes, "…we are hard pressed to find a pejorative meaning anywhere."

It should come as no surprise then that when a church father directly comments on 1 Tim 2:12, he rules out all female authoritative-teaching, not "merely" those who were doing so in a disruptive way (as if *authentein* had an exclusively pejorative sense). Here is St. Chrysostom again, from his fourth homily on Titus [emphases mine],

" 'But I do not permit a woman to teach.' But listen to what Paul added: 'Nor to have authority (*authentein*) over a man.' For to men it is permitted to teach both men and women from on high; to women he permits the word of exhortation at home, but nowhere does he allow them to preside, or does he let them hold an extended discourse. For this reason he added the words, 'nor to have authority (*authentein*) over a man." (quoted in *Women in the Church*, p. 88)

POST-HISTORY PART 2:
EARLY TRANSLATIONS OF THE BIBLE

When we look at early translations of the Bible we see *authentein* in 1 Tim 2:12 being translated into words that, with only one exception (the Syriac Peshitta, which was corrected in later Syriac editions), are words that would be glossed in English as 'authority' without a pejorative sense.

The various Old Latin translations (predecessors to St. Jerome's Vulgate) render it with: *Praepositam* ("commander"), *dominare, dominari* ("lord"), *principari* ("ruler"). Jerome selected *dominari*. (I wish it didn't need to be said that the false-friend of "dominate" is not a part of the semantic range of latin's *dominari*, which is simply the word, "Lord", the most common title for Jesus in Latin, and in patristic Christian latin, takes on a flavor of servant-leadership)

Sahidic Coptic: *erjoeis* ("lord"); Boharic Coptic: *ethreserjoj* ("lord"), etc. (Wolters, 85)

When Bible translations were abounding in the fourth and fifth centuries, Christian scholars began to realize the need for lexica and dictionaries, to assist the effort. One of the most prestigious of these early lexica was produced by no less a luminary than St. Cyril of Alexandria (375-444). So, what gloss does he give under the entry for *authentein*? Here it is:

N.T. *A8259: αὐθεντεῖν : Ἐξουσιάζειν (*Exousiazein, Exousia*) 1 Tim 2:12. (quoted in Hesychius, cited by Wolters, 88)

So St. Cyril would answer Fr. McCaulley's rhetorical question, "What is the difference between that word (*authentein*) and the more common ἐξουσία?" by saying "There isn't an important difference."

In sum then, the post-history of *authentein* further solidifies consensus critical scholarship of today, that *authentein* does not have a pejorative sense, and therefore, we cannot mirror-read a disruptive-teaching into the Ephesian setting to which 1 Tim 2:12 is being written. Therefore, the prohibition of women "teaching and *authentein*" is a simple prohibition of wielding authority by means of authoritative teaching generally.

CONCLUSION

If the above argument about the non-uniqueness of Ephesus and the non-pejorative meaning of *authentein* is sound and acceptable, then it appears that the Biblical command in 1 Timothy 2:12 "I do not permit a woman to teach or to exercise authority over a man" is to be understood in its plain sense, and that it is binding upon the universal Church. This is God's command to his Church. Receiving this, since it is one of the essential functions of priest to teach with authority (I leave apart here, the question of what is intended in the deaconal ordination, a topic for a future time), for the Anglican Church to ordain women to the priesthood is to go against the commands of God.

HOLY ORDERS AND PROPHETS

B. Jefferies

2020

INTRODUCTION

Why does the Church not practice the baptism for the dead, as mentioned in 1 Cor 15:29? Mormons do, of course, but why don't Christians? It is, after all, right there in the Bible, so perhaps this is something that has gotten lost in the course of history, and needs to be recovered? No, of course not. I am obviously trying to make a rhetorical point: That the Church has always relied on the reception-history of the Scripture as the central lens through which the Scripture should be read, as it pertains to the life of the Church.

We don't baptize for the dead now, because the Church has never baptized for the dead, outside of this isolated mention by St. Paul. In like manner, when we read in 1 Cor 11:5 that women/wives are to cover their heads when they pray or prophesy, according to the same principles used when it comes to baptism for the dead, we cannot take this isolated instance in Scripture and — rejecting all of the Church's reception-history — claim from this instance that this is a practice that the Church has "lost" and needs to be "recovered", and further use this argument to buttress support for the ordination of women to the priesthood.

But this is precisely the interpretive approach that proponents of Women's Ordination (WO) take when interpreting 1 Corinthians. Apart from the question of the meaning of the word *authentein* in 1 Tim 2:12, there is a second main line of argumentation that proponents of WO take based on 1 Corinthians 11:5, that, if held, can *appear* to undermine the definitive traditional teaching of 1 Tim 2.

1 Cor 11:5 simply states "Every wife/woman who prays or prophesies with her head uncovered disgraces her head." It is argued (or assumed) by pro-WO scholars that the mention in this verse of women prophesying forces us to understand prohibitions on women speaking authoritatively in Church (such as in 1 Cor 14:34, as well as 1 Tim 2:12) in a way other than their plain sense suggests. If it were the case that 1 Cor 11:5 is a reference to what we would today recognize as a female preacher, then we would be forced into such a hermeneutical puzzle, but, as I shall seek to demonstrate in this essay, 1 Cor 11:5 is in fact in perfect harmony with the traditional interpretation of the New Testament's prohibition of women as authoritative preachers. Subsequently, if we submit to this harmony, then it follows as a matter of course that the Great Tradition of the catholic Church which has omitted women as candidates for the priesthood has been right all along, just as it has been right to omit baptizing for the dead.

The positive content of 1 Cor 11:5 fails to support women's ordination when two careful distinctions in the Biblical text are recognized: (1) The distinction between various forms of prophecy and (2) The distinction of implied setting between 1 Cor 11 and 1 Cor 14.

OF VARIOUS FORMS OF PROPHECY

It is a standard fallacy (that all training in hermeneutics warns against) to assume that where the same word (lexeme) is used, the same meaning is intended in each instance. As long ago as Origen (d. 253), scholars have noted this,

> "instances of equivocal scriptural terms, such as confuse readers who suppose that because the word is the same the meaning must be the same wherever it is found…. The reader of the Divine Scripture must therefore carefully observe that the Scriptures do not invariably use the same words to denote the same things; and they make the change sometimes on account of the equivocal sense of a word, sometimes for the sake of the figurative meaning, and sometimes because the context requires a different nuance in some places from that which the word has in others." (The Philokalia of Origen, IX)

For instance, when we see the word 'tongue' (Glossa) in the New Testament, it can variously mean:

1. The literal muscle inside the mouth (e.g. Mark 7:33)
2. The words someone is saying (e.g. Rom 14:11)
3. A language, naturally acquired by the speaker (e.g. Rev 5:9)

4. The ability to communicate in a foreign-language, super-naturally acquired (e.g. Acts 2:4)
5. Glossolalia in the form of what linguists call "free vocalization" and which our pentecostal brothers call "speaking in tongues" (e.g. 1 Cor 14:2)

St. Paul can refer to both (4) and (5) when he refers to the various kinds of tongues that can be given as a Spiritual gift. There remain one or two ambiguous cases (such as Acts 10:46: Was Cornelius speaking a foreign-language, or worshiping God with free-vocalization?), but in most instances, we can distinguish the specific (different) meaning that is intended by the same word (lexeme).

Since 'tongues' and 'prophecy' function as a sort of dyad in 1 Corinthians (e.g. in 1 Cor 14), it is unsurprising that we have a similar situation when it comes to the word 'prophesy' (Greek προφητεύω: *Propheteuo*) and its cognates (prophet, prophecy). It is used in different senses, but all usages have this in common: A verbal utterance that is thought to be inspired by the Holy Spirit. These utterances could be:

1. Fore-telling the future
   (like Agabus in Acts 21:11)
2. The writings of the Prophets that came before Christ
   (e.g. Romans 1:2)
3. For the edification of the gathered local Church
   (e.g. 1 Cor 14:3)

And they could be spoken by:

1. People who were given 'prophet' as sort of epithet
   (e.g. Agabus, or as in Eph 2:20)

2. Anyone who occasionally does so, such as the four daughters of Philip, who are recorded as sometimes prophesying, but are not given the epithet of 'prophet'
(Acts 21:9)
3. Pagan sages who happened to be accurate
(e.g. Titus 1:12)

I am sure additional and finer categories could be introduced, but this suffices to show some of the diversity in the usage of the self-same word prophet.

The real question then is, when 1 Cor 11:5 assumes women "praying and prophesying", what is the nature of the activity that is signified by the word in this particular instance?

THE IMPLIED SETTING OF 1 CORINTHIANS 14

It is common for pro-WO scholars to give a sketch-outline of a possible context for the on-the-ground situation that 1 Cor 14 is written into: Wives being aggressive and disruptive, destroying the orderliness of the Corinthian Church, and whom Paul silences in their particular case, for order's sake. This is a standard take, often supported by footnotes to Witherington's 1991 Monograph *Women in the Earliest Churches*, possibly Wire and Fiorenza; corroborated by parallel cases examined by Kroeger & Kroeger and Westfall.

But what gives scholars this idea in the first place? It is a tenuous reconstruction, in the constructing of it, but then it is relied on as solid ground. Here is a quote from a recent pro-WO scholar's blog (Fr. Esau McCaulley). Note the number of hesitating modifiers (emphasis mine):

It is *possible* that there were women who were interrupting the prophetic utterances...As to why Paul would single out women in this context, this *could have* arisen due to the limited educational opportunities available to women in the first century.... Thus, they *might not* be aware of the proper mode of interaction...This call to reserve questions for home *may have* arisen from the fact that wives *might have been* participating in the evaluations of their own husband's prophesies.

On the one hand, scholarly moderation is a virtue, but on the other hand, how many layers of "mights" and "possibles" can be tolerated before the proposed scenario is rendered altogether the work of creative historical-fiction?

Do we have any data immediately pertinent to first-century Mediterranean life that suggests this scenario that has become the stock-in-trade of (most) modern biblical scholarship? The closest thing I can think of would be the data on the "New Woman", who was certainly a flaunter of gender mores, but do we have record of them ever aggressively opposing their husbands in the public sphere? We do not.

In addition, the taking of social liberties has always been a luxury afforded mostly by the very rich, not the lower classes of society, who we know comprised the bulk of the Corinthian church (1 Cor 1:26). The scenario sketched by Fr. McCaulley (and Witherington, etc.) is indeed possible, but is it probable? Does the text itself suggest, let alone demand that the simple word "to speak" (λαλεῖν: *lalein*) in 1 Cor 14:34 be translated with the highly unusual "interrogate" (so, Witherington) or "sift" (so, Thistleton) or "interrupt" (so, McCaulley)? It does not. However decadent Roman sexual morality was in Corinth, it was not therefore a bedlam of libertines — it only appears libertine to us observing it from our present semi-Christian societal mores. On the contrary, even Corinthians were neck-deep in the honor-shame culture of the first century. We cannot neglect this fact in favor of a *sui generis* mirror-reading of wives who — per McCaulley et al. — had no shame whatsoever. Such a reading may be possible, but it stretches the imagination beyond the breaking point of what is probable.

It is worth noting that the only textual evidence that prompts anything other than a "plain sense" reading of 1 Cor 14:34 (*"The women should keep silent in the Churches, for they are not permitted to speak…"*) is the mention of women prophesying in 1 Cor 11:4, from which all the "possibilities" for 1 Cor 14:34 are engendered.

(As an aside, *pace*, Gordon Fee's commentary in NICNT, the red herring of 1 Cor 14:34 as an inauthentic textual interpolation was put to rest forever by Thistleton, building on the immense work of Wire (1990) and Niccum (1997))[2]

THE IMPLIED SETTING OF 1 CORINTHIANS 11

1 Corinthians 7:1—11:16 is written primarily with a household setting in view. 1 Cor 7 is counsel about marriage,

---

[2] Anthony Thistleton, *The First Epistle to the Corinthians*. NIGTC, Eerdmans, 2000, 1148-9, "Niccum's pages are packed with powerful and succinct arguments which prove convincing."

which is by definition a domestic matter. 1 Cor 8:1-6 is about food, which is purchased in the temple-adjacent markets (cf. 1 Cor 10:25), with a brief foray into temple-"restaurants", which are forbidden. 1 Cor 9 is chiefly about the household finances and the support of apostles' domestic needs. 1 Cor 10 exhorts against idols generally, and the section summary starting at 10:23 brings it back around to a home setting. E.g. Verse 27: If an unbeliever invites you to a meal and you are disposed to go, eat whatever is set before you without raising any question on the ground of conscience.

1 Cor 11 begins as a continuation of the setting established at the end of chapter 10 (recalling that the chapter divisions are not original), I.e. a household-type gathering (which, recall, was more than the nuclear family of the 20th century, but included near kin, servants, etc.), possibly at a neighbors' house (cf. 10:27) or with guests over, and in that setting Paul exhorts:

Any woman who prays or prophesies with her head unveiled disgraces her head. (1 Cor 11:5)

Twelve verses later (11:17), Paul will then introduce his next teaching (on the Lord's supper), and he begins that section by saying:

But in the following instructions I do not commend you, because when you come together it is not for the better but for the worse. For, in the first place, when you come together as a church...

The opening word here is the sequential/contrasting conjunction δέ (*de*), which, coupled with the prefatory remark that follows ("in the following instructions") indicates a shift in the setting which Paul wants to bring to mind, in order to speak into. A setting he names very explicitly, "when you come together as a church" (11:18). This strongly suggests that the previous content of 11:1-16 is taking place in a setting other than "when you come together as a church."

It is surprising that commentators do not pay more attention to this rhetorical shift, as it relates to the big picture of interpreting the message of 1 Corinthians as a whole. Thistleton (NIGTC) dismisses it without argument but merely appeals to C.K. Barrett's 1968 commentary as a ground,[3] but Barrett himself makes an assertion with no evidence for why a change of setting should not be considered when trying to reconcile the prohibition of 1 Cor 14:34 with the reference to women "prophesying" in 11:5.[4]

But a rhetorical shift there certainly is, and this is the key that unlocks the puzzle of how 1 Cor 11 and 1 Cor 14 are harmonious. Attempts by NT scholars of a more "feminist" persuasion (Fee, Witherington, etc.), despite whatever cautions they lay down in the process, end up forcing 1 Cor 14:34 to sound like it is saying something quite different than the strong, clear, un-caveated injunction that it is. If the "real meaning" of "The women should keep silent in the Churches, for they are not permitted to speak…" is actually

---

[3] Thistleton, NIGTC, 1156

[4] C.K. Barrett, *The First Epistle to the Corinthians*, BNTC, A&C Black, 1968, under 14:34-35: "there is nothing to suggest either this, or that the speaking referred to in 11:5 takes place in a private house-gathering, and not in the church assembly."

"Wives are not allowed to rudely interrogate their husbands", the question is begged: Why didn't Paul say that? Why did he give the larger, wider command? And why speak with such a forceful appeal by referring to "all the churches" (v.33b)? Even if the potentially-possible situation reconstructed by Witherington et al. were the case on the ground, it would appear that 14:34 remains nothing less than an instance of the characteristically Pauline move of offering a generalized teaching out of the prompt of a particular circumstance.

Apart from pre-textual feminist commitments, the felt-need to make such exegetical contortions apparently comes from reading the mentioning of women prophesying in 11:5 apart from the two pertinent pieces of data I have brought forward: The way 'to prophesy' can mean different things, and the different setting in which it is happening. If 11:5 is thought to be taking place "at church",[5] then 14:34 can't mean what it sounds like — for how could they "be silent" if they are permitted to prophesy? But this problem resolves itself when the fact of the shift in implied setting is recognized.

PUTTING IT ALL TOGETHER

One species of 'prophecy' is authoritative teaching in the gathered assembly (ἐκκλησία). This is the prophecy that is

---

[5] Of course, prior to A.D. 313 church "buildings" were few and far between, and most churches gathered in homes. But there still would have been a clear and recognizable difference between when the assembly was gathered (such as on the Lord's day, Acts 20:7), and when Christian households were informally "hanging out" together. This latter is the setting of 1 Cor 11, and the former of 1 Cor 14.

the object of discussion through the entirety of 1 Cor 14. It is known thus by its effect: "the one who prophesies speaks to people for their upbuilding and encouragement and consolation." (v. 3) and it is plainly exercised in the gathered assembly: "If, therefore, the whole church comes together and all speak in tongues, and outsiders or unbelievers enter, will they not say that you are out of your minds? But if all prophesy, and an unbeliever or outsider enters, he is convicted by all." (v.23-24)

What Paul and the Corinthian church called 'prophecy' as the word is used in 1 Cor 14, we would today call 'preaching'. Indeed, this has been the traditional interpretation of 1 Cor 14 for a long time, to equate 'prophecy' (in this context) with 'preaching' as near synonyms (vide. St. Thomas Aquinas, "So he [Paul] calls teachers and preachers 'prophets'...").[6]

The New Testament states with a single voice that a prophet-preacher in the gathered assembly must be a man (e.g. 1 Cor 14:34, 1 Tim 2:12, Titus 1:5-9). It is very interesting that in the New Testament, while women are mentioned as prophesying (e.g. Acts 11:5, Acts 21:9), no woman is ever called "a prophet", as a noun. This is suggestive of more than accidental language-use, rather, "prophet" was seen to be both a recipient of the charism of prophecy, and an authorized role in the Church. This conception is corroborated by the appearance of "prophets" in the list in Ephesians 4:11.

---

[6] St. Thomas Aquinas' sermon on the Feast of Sts. Peter & Paul, available in translation online at https://isidore.co/aquinas/english/SermAttendite.htm

However, the ministry of prophecy exercised by an authorized prophet is only one of the forms of the charism of prophecy can take. This brings us back around to the question I posed earlier about 1 Cor 11:5 (and Acts 21:9, etc) — what were the women who prophesied doing? They were uttering Holy Spirit inspired speech, certainly, just not in the midst of the gathered Church. This is much easier to imagine on this side of the pentecostal movement in the 20th century: The Gifts of the Spirit are not confined to be used only in the gathered assembly, they can be used at any time, as the Spirit empowers.

That 11:5 is an instance of this outside-of-church prophetic-speech is given additional support by the fact that the speech-act that is being referenced is referred to eight verses later as simply 'prayer' — "...is it proper for a woman to pray to God with her head uncovered?" (11:13) Prayer, of course, is not confined to the assembly, but just like certain kinds of prophesy, could be exercised "wherever two or three are gathered."

Clearly, there was a small informal gathering (How else could Paul have found out about it?) in which prayer and prophecy took place, with a woman who did so without her head covered. Indexed onto the ecclesial landscape of today, it could have been a mere gathering of friends, or perhaps a "small-group". Either way, it is the presence of other believers that prompts Paul to re-enforce the "properness" (11:13) of head-covering for Christian women when prophesying/praying.

Scholars are divided as to whether the head-covering Paul enjoins is long hair that is "down", or the traditional greco-roman hood-type veil (think of the one Mary is always portrayed as wearing in Icons),[7] but the meaning of abandoning either is very similar, since both acts would convey an air of worldliness. Either an elaborate "up" hair-style such as mentioned also in 1 Tim 2:9 that would communicate decadence or profligacy, or simply un-covered hair that would have been a fashion among the "New Women" of the era, but acted against the mores and sensibilities of ordinary society in which a married woman's hair was always covered outside of her private chambers.

The issue of a Christian woman having her head covered then, apart from the theological rationale that Paul offers (11:4-16), is simply one of integrity: To not be speaking in the power of God about the world-denying Gospel of Christ, while outwardly presenting in a very worldly way. A rough analogy would be if a Christian woman today were to be talking prophetically about self-denial while wearing huge diamond earrings, or giving an exhortation to friends about purity, while wearing a rather immodest outfit. It is the incongruity that prompts Paul to remind the women of Corinth about the traditions he delivered (1 Cor 11:1), which keep the Church standing apart from the worldliness of the world, either in how worldly women are presenting themselves inappropriately (to the sensitivities of most), or how worldly men covered their heads with a hood when offering sacrifices to pagan roman deities.

It is sometimes pointed out that since a hood-veil was only enjoined culturally upon married women, as it is in chapter

---

[7] See the excellent summary of the scholarship in Thistleton, NIGTC, 823-832

11, and that since the conclusion to the prohibition in 14:34 is v. 35 — "…let them ask their husbands at home" — and of course, an unmarried woman has no husband to ask, therefore the ambiguous greek word in 1 Cor 14:34 γυνή (*gune*) should be understood here only as 'wives' and not 'women' generally. The implication of this is that unmarried women may not have fallen under the prohibition of 1 Cor 14:35, and therefore unmarried women may not have been silent when the Church gathered in Corinth. If this were the case, then indeed there would not be a univocal New Testament witness against women preachers in Church, and we would have a mixed set of data from which to discern. However this interpretive swan-song, like the hypothesized "interrogating wives" reconstruction, has no traction on the ground of the first century. As Barrett writes in his commentary on 1 Cor 14:35,

"The verse [35] contemplates married women, whose husbands are Christians. A fortiori, unmarried women and the wives of unbelievers will not speak in the assembly; if they wish to learn they must presumably persuade married friends to put questions to their husbands." [8]

CONCLUSION

Upon closer analysis of the contextual setting of 1 Corinthians 11 and 14, it is clear that the kind of prophetic speech offered by women that is referenced in 1 Cor 11:5 is different than the kind that is offered exclusively by men in 1 Cor 14 in the

---

[8] Barrett, Loc. Cit., 1 Cor 14:35

midst of official church gatherings. Put another way, women can prophesy, but this does not mean, according to NT usage, that they are prophets. The difference in kind is strongly suggested by the shift in setting that occurs after Paul has addressed the women prophesying (in 11:5), in 11:17, when the gathered Church is brought into view, and into which the prohibition of 1 Cor 14:34 is given. 1 Cor 11:5 therefore provides no mitigation against the strong prohibition in 1 Cor 14:34, "the women should keep silent in the churches," which for 1900 years was interpreted as having the same meaning as 1 Tim 2:12: That women cannot be authoritative preachers in the one holy catholic and apostolic Church.

Indexed onto our Anglican setting, this means that the Bible prohibits women being ordained to the priesthood, since authoritative preaching is one of the principle functions of that order.

THE PROBLEM WITH MAKING A PATRISTIC ARGUMENT FOR THE ORDINATION OF WOMEN: A RESPONSE TO EMILY MCGOWIN

L. Nelson

2019

Emily McGowin has made an argument for the ordination of women to the priesthood.[1] This is, as she notes, a limited argument, not meant in any way to be a comprehensive defense. It involves a pseudo-patristic Christological argument as follows: if the incarnation of Our Lord assumed not just male human nature but human nature more generally (including both male and female), then both men and women can be saved. And, therefore, both men and women can represent the incarnate Christ as priests.

The first inference was made explicitly by Gregory of Nazianzus and other Fathers. The second was drawn by none of the Fathers.

As the argument proceeds from Patristic Christology, and as the Fathers were writing as interpreters of Holy Scripture,

---

McGowin, Emily, 'If Women Can Be Saved, Then Women Can Be Priests: A Critique of the "in persona Christi" Argument Against Women's Ordination' published on AnglicanCompass.com (Sep 2019)

her innovative argument must be subject to biblical scrutiny. And being subject to biblical scrutiny, it fails. Let me try to explain why.

That both men and women can be saved by our common Redeemer is a basic Christian belief. All of the baptized share in a royal priesthood: "You are a chosen race, a royal priesthood, a holy nation, God's own people, that you may declare the wonderful deeds of him who called you out of darkness into his marvelous light." (1 Peter 2:9)

But we must remember that the first Christians were Jews. They knew that all Israelites were called to be part of a priestly nation (Ex. 19:6), but that God called only a select number of men to be priests as a special vocation (Ex 21& 22).

So too, in the Church, we are all called to live in a priestly manner, but only a few are called to the vocation of priesthood. All Christians act in a priestly manner as they live out their vocation within the created order. Every act, whether it's brewing coffee, or feeding your children, or working as a doctor, or feeding the poor, even just walking down the street, becomes a priestly act if it is carried out prayerfully and in witness to Jesus. But this is a reality wholly distinct from how we ought to think about ordination.

Anglicans have a deeply rooted theological method. We start with Scripture, taking it in its plain and canonical sense, respectful of the Church's consensual and historic reading (e.g. the Jerusalem Declaration). If something cannot be proven by Holy Scripture, it cannot be required to be believed because, as we put it, Scripture contains all things necessary to salvation.

Then we look to the tradition, specifically how the Church has read Scripture. From there, we exercise right reason to answer the question before us, bound again by Holy Scripture and the consensual readings which we find in the Tradition.

The Fathers understand themselves to be bearers of the very faith they had received in Holy Scripture. They carry out this tradition, not in abstraction from Scripture but in conformity to it. Another way of putting it is this: for Christians, logic has a name: Jesus Christ, as he is revealed in Holy Scripture, as he is testified to down through the centuries, and as we have received him.

One of the biggest problems with McGowin's argument is that she does not start with Scripture. Instead, she starts with a questionable patristic argument (with which the Fathers she quotes would not have agreed) and then builds from that to attempt to tell us why we must accept this dramatic change in teaching and practice.

McGowin's failure to robustly engage Scripture first shows up when she assumes that men and women can represent Christ and the Church equally (or equally badly, as the case may be)—either analogously, iconographically, or sacramentally. She reasons that if male and female can be saved, then male and female can function more or less equally. This reasoning, of course, has the benefit of widely received notions in the culture that support her. But what she doesn't have is the backing of Holy Scripture.

We see in Genesis that woman is drawn out of the side of the man, and fashioned from one of the man's ribs (Gen. 2:21-22). Human nature is created first in Adam, and while

Eve's human nature is full, it is of a derivative sort. While man and woman are both made in the image of God, we see that they are set to carry out very different vocations within the created order.

The woman relates to all living as life-giver and mother. All human life will now come forth from a woman. The man's relation to creation is that of a father and gardener, tending the garden and bringing forth life from the ground. While they exhibit what John Paul II called a "somatic homogeneity"—meaning that their bodies are of the same substance—their sexual difference serves to show the relation between God and creation: one gives and the other receives.

The New Testament witness is similar. While soteriological distinctions between man and woman pass away in baptism (Galatians 3:28), men and women retain distinctions in the ways they serve the divine economy.

Paul writes, "The head of every man is Christ, the head of a woman is her husband, and the head of Christ is God" (1 Cor. 11:3). He does "not permit a woman to teach or to have authority over men" (1 Tim. 2:12). Distinctions of dress and conduct within the Church between men and women are maintained, even while they are "joint heirs of the grace of life" (1 Pet. 3:7).

So while the sacrament of baptism unites man and woman in a redeemed humanity, it does not erase bodily distinctions or hierarchies of authority within the Church. Just as the one-flesh union of marriage does not erase sexual distinction, but puts that distinction to sacramental use to show forth the mystical union between Christ and his Church, so the union of man and woman in one Church means that their sexual difference is not reduced but enhanced. Their ontological status as redeemed children before God is the same, but they do not fulfill the same functions, or even show forth the same realities in living that redeemed life.

Women and men have different ways of serving the Lord Christ, as do parents and children, pastors and their flocks. Sacramental order and the orders of ministry exhibit hierarchies that allow men and women to exercise their unique roles in showing forth the glory of the Church's Incarnate head.

The New Testament, while affirming the ministry of women in various forms, leaves no room for women to be ordained as either presbyters or as bishops. Arguments to the contrary are must turn Scriptures on their head to make them fit desired conclusions.

But at no point do the New Testament authors surmise from this that women cannot be saved! They simply teach that some roles are reserved for women and others for men. The question of whether or not women can image forth the Incarnation in the person of Christ is unanswered by the New Testament authors. What they do answer is the question of whether a woman may have authority over a man and whether a woman can or should serve the Church as a sacramental sign of Christ as a priest or a bishop. The answer is no.

Therefore, McGowin's argument cannot be taken seriously by anyone who takes the authority of Scripture seriously.

This method of reasoning is also vulnerable to the theological and exegetical method of liberal Protestantism: determine the alteration to faith and practice which must be made in order to survive or thrive in the modern world, develop an exegetical or theological method to suit that end, and conduct whatever pyrotechnics are necessary to effect that change.

In fact, such an argument in its literal reading could be applied to suit just about any alteration to the Church's historic teachings on sex, the role of men and women, or marriage.

Now, I don't accuse her of proposing any of that. But this method, if applied consistently, would lead to wholesale alteration of the Church's teaching, in defiance of Scripture. This, alas, is the problem of exalting so-called logic over divine revelation in Scripture.

Ironically, I think that McGowin's argument actually shows why only a man can represent both sexes before God as a priest. For she accepts the fact that the man Jesus can adequately redeem both men and women. It stands to reason that if one (albeit divine) man can best redeem both sexes, another man can well represent both sexes at the altar.

Furthermore, it makes eminent sense for a man—and not a woman—to stand for Jesus at the altar saying "This is my [man's] Body given for you." Yet McGowin has strangely directed the reader to the all-embracing humanity of Jesus Christ the God-Man, and then misdirected the reader to the "logical" conclusion that a male-only presbyterate cannot adequately represent its flock at the altar. It is even more strange to suggest that a woman can play the role of a king, much less our heavenly King.

Bear with me a bit more as I examine her syllogism.

> The Incarnate Christ, as male, represents and redeems humanity, both male and female.
> Women can be redeemed.
> Therefore, women can be priests.

Her conclusion is a non sequitur because it involves a very serious category error, the blurring of the distinction between soteriology and sacramentology which occurs between the second premise and the conclusion.

McGowin claims two things. First, that the distinctions between men and women are non-essential (thus rejecting the essentialism that God himself invented and reveals in Scripture, endorsed by the Fathers), and therefore non-essential to how we think about sacramental order.

Second, she argues that the ability of male and female bodies to serve sacramentally to image forth the Incarnate Christ are equally (in)sufficient.

McGowin anticipates the response that redemption and sacramental representation are different. Indeed. I would say that not only are these categories different, but ignoring that difference is at the heart of McGowin's argument. Clearly, the idea that a woman can be saved and the idea that a woman can be ordained a priest are two different ideas, borne out by the fact that not all Christians are ordained. The argument is something akin to saying "Birds can fly, therefore feathers can fly." She confuses the properties of the whole Church with the properties of a part. But, McGowin doesn't take this distinction between categories seriously. By blurring the categories, McGowin sets the ground for her argument, but alas, this category error is its fatal flaw.

McGowin responds that "an analogy does not require a pure one-to-one correspondence." That is emphatically true. If it is true that God can only be known by analogy, then that is all we have, imperfect similarities that always fall short. There is even a question in Christian theology as to whether or not God can ever be known in his essence at all. The idea is that we can only ever "tell the truth, but tell it slant" (to use Emily Dickinson's phrase).

But, this is an activity wholly dissimilar from McGowin's proposal: that man and woman as analogues to Christ are equally bad, and being equally bad, should be equally embraced. Yet the argument made by those who hold that only a male priest can stand in the place of Christ sacramentally is not saying that the analogy is perfect, only that it is fitting, and being fitting, only a male priesthood can sign forth Christ who is Incarnate as a man, and as such the savior and redeemer of all mankind, both male and female.

Christian theology does not throw up its hands and say "Well, all analogies fall short, therefore we should stop trying" but rather, "All analogies fall short, some more than others. Therefore every attempt should be made to be as precise as possible." Analogies, in order to be helpful in lending clarity, must fit. They must lead us closer to the truth, not away from it.

McGowin asserts that "sacramental representation means the priest functions not as Christ, but as an icon of Christ." She argues, with William Witt, that physical similarity to the male body of Christ is not central, but without saying why it is not. They seem to mean that both male and female bodies can function semiotically to point to Christ. As I have said, when it comes to the notion of the Church functioning in this way ecclesially as Bride to point to Christ, that is absolutely the case. But our symbols matter. As Ken Myers continually reminds us, "Matter matters." Why did Jesus choose for his symbols twelve men? Why not one of the Marys? McGowin does not wrestle with this.

McGowin proposes that the sacramental image of the priest is conformity to the pattern of Christ, the Suffering Servant, which though not defined, can be understood to mean that insofar as the priest suffers, or serves, or prays, only then is Christ represented.

But it was Donatism which taught that the priest must be a moral or spiritual exemplar in order to be effective as a sacramental sign. The Church has taught consistently that it is actually in doing what the Church does, that the priest functions sacramentally.

And if that is the case—and the tradition says that it is—how can anyone claiming to be a priest do what the Church has not done? How can it be that this powerful sacramental sign of Christ's Incarnate priesthood be so dramatically altered (a process not wholly different from a sex change) without dramatically altering our fundamental convictions concerning Christ himself?

In order for an icon to "work," it must participate in that which it images forth. While there can be little doubt that a woman can image forth Christ due to her participation in him, what is in question is whether a woman can image forth Christ giving us his Body and Blood as she presides over the Church, specifically in the celebration of the Eucharist.

McGowin claims that both male and female bodies can function sacramentally to represent either the Church or Christ. The main assertion is that if a male body can represent Christ at the altar and also represent the female Bride, then women can fulfill both ordained functions as well. But this does not follow.

First, while it is freely admitted that women can represent Christ, this is not the question. The question is whether or not women can be ordained as presbyters in the Church to preside over the Eucharistic assembly, representing Christ, who is the head of the Body. Can women exercise this authority? She claims that these sexual differences do not show us anything essential, that we must look past sexual difference to see bare humanity in a more general sense, as if anyone could do so. Yet the scandal and power of the Incarnation are found precisely in its particularity—that Christ was incarnate, not as an androgynous human being, but as a man.

McGowin's last assertion, however, needs to be challenged most vigorously: that those "who feast at Eucharistic tables presided over by women priests get to see glimpses of this new creation every Sunday."

The claim is essentially this: that an all-male priesthood is deficient, and again, if this is the case in the Church, then why is it not the case with Christ? How have we not become captive to what C.S. Lewis termed "chronological snobbery," the idea that we, in our late times, have finally put a finger on the truth, that we now understand so much more than our predecessors in the faith? What can account for this discrepancy? Sexism? Misogyny?

And how on earth is one supposed to deflect those accusations from Our Lord himself? How can the appointment of twelve male apostles be anything but the sin of sexism, blinding the Church intentionally from seeing the full picture of the new creation? And lastly, what of the status of women who attend churches that only have male priests, including large parts of Anglicanism, the Roman Catholic Church, and the Orthodox Churches? Do they not, by participating fully in the liturgy, show forth Christ's new creation every Sunday? Do they not get to see glimpses of redemption?

McGowin's central claim was that men and women are interchangeable—which Scripture and history and biology deny. But at the end of her article we get to this last, additional, claim–that the inclusion of women in the presbyterate provides us with something vastly superior.

By asserting an imposed vision that is considered not a development of, but as superior to, the biblical and historical vision of man and woman, and by blurring the lines between soteriology and sacramentology, McGowin has undermined and disparaged the very theology and practice of the Fathers which she has claimed to defend. This patristic theology is not only deeply biblical, but for that very reason and its attestation by the Fathers, it is authoritative for us as Anglicans.

IMAGO DEI, PERSONA CHRISTI

A. Wilgus

2019

The debate touched off by Emily Mcgowin's article on Women's Orders in Anglican Pastor has opened onto the vast territory of the theology of gender. That is, of course, an important controversy to have out (though perhaps not on comment boards), but in the midst of the ruckus, I think that it is worth returning to her original argument, which was a good deal narrower in scope and worth treating on its own merits because it presents a good opportunity to talk about sacraments, what we think they are, and how we reason about them. She makes the case that the doctrine of *In Persona Christi* (the idea that the priest stands in the representation of Christ at the altar), though frequently cited by gender traditionalists, actually supports the possibility of a female priesthood. If Christ, though male, saved women by his assumption of their common humanity, then that humanity ought to be good enough to represent him at the altar.

Though this is an attractive argument, this is not where the logic of *In Persona Christi* comes from, and the reality is not nearly so complicated. The doctrine, like all good sacramental theology, proceeds from the same experience that you instinctively have when you are viewing or drawing a picture of Jesus. It doesn't matter if it is an Orthodox icon or a Sunday School coloring book: the best way to represent Christ is as a male because Christ was male.

If this seems too obvious that's because I think it is. Sacraments are pictures after all, and talking about pictures requires a vocabulary that may seem unsatisfactory when it comes to systematic theology, but it is actually part of the foundations of our theology. The sacraments are revealed images, and we reason from them, not to them.

What about the controversy between those who believe female ordination is possible and those who don't: why would two different pictures inspire such heated debate and threat of division? This is because sacraments are not just ordinary images. A sacrament is a symbol that does what it says it does. It's like the difference between a wedding ring (a ring does not make you married) and a signature on a contract (you're bound to this now). A sacrament is called an effective sign because the sign accomplishes what it signifies. Because sacraments are effective signs, the form of the symbol is not interchangeable. In short, the matter matters. Changing the image changes what it does.

McGowin rightly points out that sacraments, like icons, don't require one-to-one correspondence. But that does not mean that they do not require any correspondance. An "analogy of being" needs to make sense, after all. The comparison McGowin makes to icons is particularly helpful here since the tradition of Eastern icon painting comes with very strict rules about what sorts of innovations the artist may or may not make–and deviations from these tropes have even been denounced as spiritually dangerous! So like icons, it is important to know whether we have the right picture in our sacraments. Where do we turn to find out?

To answer: let us take another example from the sacrament of the Eucharist. How do we know that bread must be the picture for Christ's body and not another form of grain like breakfast cereal? Where do we look? This is where scripture and the Church's tradition (the faithful witness to scripture) is our guide. The scriptures tell us that Jesus identified bread as his body. If we aren't sure we got that right, we look at the practice of the early Church and we see that, indeed, we got the same message from it as its earliest hearers. When sacramental Anglicans refer to "the universal practice of the undivided Church" we aren't swinging a club, we're asking: "does what we hear from the scriptures agree with its earliest hearers?" When things seem unclear or there appears to be some wiggle room, then we feel authorized to agree to disagree. But when our ideas disagree to the point of contradiction with the overwhelming witness of the early Church then we need to check our hearing. If the earliest Christians used bread, if they used bread everywhere, if all orthodox Christians used bread, then we should really not use something else. Because the bread in the sacrament is an effective sign, then that means that having bread is essential to receiving Christ's body, and we are not authorized to go about it any other way.

Before we get to where I'm obviously going (and while you may be marshaling your objections), let's take a moment so that we do not miss something important. Without the scripture and the Church's practice, there is no way that we could have ever figured out that bread is how we receive Christ's body. Our reason rightly takes a back seat to what has been revealed. But that does not mean that God's choice makes no sense. Looking through the scriptures, we see that God has often used bread to represent spiritual sustenance and administer real sustenance: The priest Melchizedek brings out bread (and wine) to Abraham, God gives Israel the manna in the wilderness, there is the mysterious "bread of the presence" in the tabernacle, there is Elijah's miraculous meal on the way to Horeb, and Elisha's multiplied barley loaves. Christ himself multiplied bread at his feeding miracles–events which clearly looked forward to the Eucharist. These do not explain why Christ's flesh could not have been represented by something else, but it is easy to see why it makes sense that it is, and we can then safely turn to theology to discern and debate God's reasons for this. But I do not believe that we are capable of coming up with a different picture than the revealed one.

So how is it that maleness is an essential quality of standing *In Persona Christi* and, say, Jewishness, being 33 years old, bearded, and having (probably) brown eyes and skin are not? What does it actually take to render Christ's form faithfully at the altar, to stand *In Persona Christi*? These are not impious questions, and I am glad that folks are asking them. Here again, scripture must be our guide. When it came time to replace Judas the apostate from among the twelve, no facial, racial, or any other accidental features are mentioned, except that the new overseer must come from "one of the men who have accompanied us during all the time that the Lord Jesus went in and out among us." (Acts 1:21). It is also important to note that this is said in the presence of "the women and Mary." (Acts 1:14). Then there is Paul's famous (infamous?) anthropology of male and female roles in Church which reinforce the impression that Christ's authoritative representatives–to whom are apportioned the offices of sacramental administration and the office of teaching–in the Church are to be male. Add that to the male priesthood of Israel whom Christ re-images in his selection of his 12 disciples, all of whom are male and one gets the overwhelming impression that humanity alone is not the sign for the sacrament of Holy Orders. Male humanity is. Have we heard our scriptures clearly on this matter? Again, the early Church thinks we have. The universal practice of the Episcopal traditions–those that have ordained bishops in the apostolic lineage–has endured as a male episcopate and presbyterate ("bishop" and "priest" were interchangeable terms in the New Testament) to the present day. For this reason, it is also important to consult the other communions that have maintained the Apostolic Succession. When Rome and the East agree on something, it is a good idea to listen to what it is.

This is not to say that faithful Christians are not allowed to bring Christ's feminine qualities to light (Julian of Norwich springs to mind). But I would argue that the Church's mystical tradition has felt free to do this when it has not threatened to change his authoritative image. No amount of such mysticism ever produced a tradition of female Christs in icon or sculpture, and if the priesthood is also an "icon" of greater weight, then we ought to keep that in mind. This also goes to Dr. McGowin's point on how a mixed congregation can be rendered to be female. The male priesthood vouchsafes the female Church, for even though men appear there, women are exclusively to be found there and may justly take some pride of place, as the many images of the Virgin have attested. This is why in some Reformed Episcopal dioceses, deaconesses wear special cassocks and sit prominently interspersed around the congregation. As to McGowin's question about how the male priest may stand In Persona Ecclesiae, I would simply say that the priest stands as such toward God and not the people. Whereas God, being God, is not liable to be confused by a male representing his bride, the Church, being people, would likely be confused by Christ rendered, consistently and authoritatively, as a woman (imagine entering an Orthodox Church and the great icon of Mary and Christ over the altar (Our Lady of the Sign) is reversed: a female Christ inside of a male Mary.). But here I have joined McGowin in pious speculation. When we have received revelation as such, then we are free to wonder. What we are not free to do is change the image.

There is a good deal to be said about the importance of female leadership in the Church, but such discussions should take place on their own terms for the edification of the Church, instead of appending them to a debate on Holy Orders. It would do our sisters an indignity to treat the subject as a consolation prize. However, I should acknowledge that the above reasoning is certainly frustrating for our sisters and brothers who believe that female ordination is a possibility for a couple of understandable reasons. It seems all very neat, even circular: the picture cannot be altered into something else because then it would not be the picture. But these are the waters we must enter when we talk about any of our sacraments. They are revealed, effective images, not pictorial emanations of our best theology. Dr. McGowin, as a good confessing theologian, no doubt agrees that our soteriology must reason from revelation, but the way in which she reasons to the form of the images, indicates that she does not seem to count the sacraments as part of this latter category (and I do not think that she is alone in this). In my opinion, turning the debate about women's orders into a discussion on what sacraments really are, and therefore what we may and may not do with them, would be a most welcome development for the ACNA.

Images can be frustrating things. Indeed, this is no less true for opponents of women's orders than proponents. But Christ's own maleness presents us with the same, frustrating quandary: how can it be that Christ, the perfect image of our genderless God, appeared as a male? Is it simply that he needed to pick one out of necessity and decided to flip a coin? (or as theologians like to put it: "the incarnation meant exhibiting the quality of gendered particularity") Was he constrained by the cultural precepts of his time? Or does his revelation as the bridegroom coming for his bride carry deep significance? Whatever we reason about these questions, Christ must be received in the form in which he came, and if the priesthood is indeed to stand in his person, then it must do so as well.

SACRAMENTAL REPRESENTATION AND THE CREATED ORDER

B. Johnson

2019

In the Anglican Church in North America, the question of women's ordination to the priesthood continues to be discussed with each diocese left to decide its own practice. A recurring point of debate is how we are to understand the priest's representative role in the liturgy.

Emily McGowin, in a recent article, challenges the argument that only male priests can represent Christ (*in persona Christi*) in the celebration of the Eucharist on the basis that Christ was male.

Referring to the maxim of Gregory of Nazianzus, "For that which he has not assumed he has not healed," McGowin foregrounds this Christological formulation and its relationship to the *in persona Christi* role of the priesthood. Christ, though male, assumed and redeemed humanity, not just male humanity. Therefore, McGowin argues, since Christ shared in and redeemed humanity, women may function *in persona Christi* in the Eucharist. Notably, McGowin is not arguing against the *in persona Christi* role of the priesthood but for a more expansive understanding of it that includes female priests.

She draws out the implication of her argument:

> If women *qua* women are fundamentally incapable—and, according to some Christians, even *ontologically* incapable—of representing the male Jesus Christ in their female persons, then that calls into question whether their female persons can be redeemed by the male Jesus Christ.

McGowin surely has an important point that women *qua* women can indeed represent Christ in their female beings. Any argument for a male-only priesthood which also contends that only men can represent Christ in *any* context not only leads to the sorts of theological problems McGowin points out but undoes the whole telos of the Christian life for male and female: being transformed into the image of Christ (Rom. 8:29).

But there is a different understanding of the *in persona Christi* argument that steers clear of the dangers McGowin flags up and yet retains the symbolic and gendered character of sacramental leadership. The issue is not whether a woman can qua woman represent Christ (of course, as McGowin shows, she can). The issue is whether the body as male and female has any symbolic significance at all in a liturgical setting.

Anticipating the response that the order of redemption and sacramental representation work in a different register, McGowin poses the question: "On what basis does the concept of sacramental representation rest?"

This is a great question, and one that should push us into more thoughtful engagement with how Scripture might answer it. McGowin answers this question by way of the analogy of being: since no human, male or female, can represent Christ "exactly, literally, univocally," then women along with men can participate in persona Christ as analogues.

But it strikes me that the most important place to go in discovering the basis for our understanding of sacramental representation is the opening of Genesis. A sacramental and typological reading of the creation narrative sheds light on the question of priestly representation in a eucharistic and liturgical setting.

In Genesis 1, humanity is created male and female to bear God's image in the world (Gen.1:26-28). In this context, male and female both represent God as his image bearers in taking dominion in the world. When we zoom into Genesis chapter 2, however, we discover a sacramental context in the Garden of Eden.

Yaweh creates Adam first, places him in a garden, and gives him priestly commands "to serve and guard" the garden (Gen. 2:15). The commands given to Adam for serving and guarding are the same verbs used for the duties of priests in the service of the tabernacle in Numbers (e.g., Num. 1:53; 3:7; 8:11; 18:7). Thus Adam is created as a priest to guard and serve the prototypical garden sanctuary.

The garden is a sanctuary whose imagery is later symbolized and reduplicated in the tabernacle and temple. The garden is also a place of sacramental food, represented by the fruit-bearing trees.

From Adam's side, God builds a bride, the woman, whom we can think of a liturgical respondent in this garden sanctuary. But the priest Adam is to convey the instruction of the Lord regarding the sacramental trees to the bride. Adam is a priest tasked with teaching God's word to the bride and overseeing the sacramental food with regard to the trees. As a priestly guard, he's to do what the cherub with a flaming sword will later do: keep intruders out of the garden.

Of course, Adam the priest fails in this regard. He abdicates his priestly vocation, allowing an intruder, the serpent, into the sanctuary. This intruder goes after the bride and gets her to take the prohibited sanctuary food. She in turn takes the forbidden fruit and serves it Adam who was standing there, failing to speak God's word and allowing the deception to take place. The scene is a sort of false eucharistic meal that upends the Lord's liturgical design and commands.

Now, what does this have to do with priestly ministry in a sacramental context?

In the created order we have man and woman in a liturgical, sacramental setting. The man/husband/priest Adam has a priestly duty vis-a-vis the bride. His maleness isn't incidental in this creation context, but symbolic and representative of the human race, including the woman. Ultimately, he's a type of the Second Adam, Jesus Christ.

Jesus also has a bride formed from his side, the church. The church like Eve is both bride and liturgical respondent to Jesus, the true husband and great high priest. And the Second Adam deals with the intruder once and for all and makes a way for the church to eat from the sacramental Tree of Life.

Marriage is another context in which we can consider gendered representation. The husband represents Christ to the wife and the wife represents the church to the husband (Eph. 5:22-32). Of course, this doesn't mean the wife cannot represent Christ in any way nor the husband the church. But there is an asymmetrical calling given to the husband to play the Christ role that doesn't apply in the same way to the wife in marriage.

The nuptial mystery of Christ and his Church has been a key consideration in Roman Catholic understanding of the male priesthood. Pope Paul VI, in *Inter Insigniores*, sees the nuptial theme woven throughout Scripture and its attendant symbolism in male and female as significant liturgically. The priest is representative of Christ the Head and Christ the groom. The priest does also represent the church (*in persona ecclesiae*) but "precisely because he first represents Christ himself, who is the Head and the Shepherd of the Church."

The defense of a male-only priesthood in the Eastern Orthodox tradition has focused more on the fatherly character of the priest and not the priest operating *in persona Christi*. Still, Fr. Alexander Schmemann claims that a contemplation of the "nuptial mystery" of Christ and the Church is requisite for understanding why priests must be men.

All of this is to point out that the historic position—East and West—has not simply relied on a few proof texts or facile appeals to *in persona Christi*. Rather, the argument for a male-only priesthood lies in deep typological patterns embedded in Scripture, not least in the nuptial mystery of Christ and his Church.

The typological representation in marriage is gendered. And so it is in a liturgical context. Genesis doesn't give us a biological description of male and female, but it does give us a liturgical one. Like marriage, liturgy does not assume androgynous categories of the body, but invests male and female categories with typological significance, rooted in creation and pointing to redemption.

Too often, 1 Timothy 2:8-15 is appealed to as a simple knockdown verse against women's ordination. But what can be overlooked is why exactly Paul grounds his argument in the created order. Paul appeals to the creation context, which, as we've seen, is a context that *does* concern priestly, sacramental representation by the male. That Paul roots his argument in creation, and given the sacramental and liturgical context of the creation account, we should take seriously how sacramental representation, liturgical leadership is established in the created order.

The liturgical anthropology of Genesis 1-2, the representative and masculine nature of the Old Covenant priesthood—or even something obscure like the sex requirements for particular animal sacrifices in Leviticus 1-7—might very well be fruitful avenues of further exploration in how we think about sacramental representation in the Bible.

Dr. McGowin helpfully highlights some problems in how we can think about sacramental representation. As Anglicans continue to debate women's ordination, I hope the sorts of questions raised by her piece encourage a deeper exploration with how Scripture might re-orient us to the question of sacramental representation, liturgical leadership, and the created order.

BROTHERS, WE HAVE FAILED: A LAMENT IN RESPONSE TO THE WOMEN'S ORDINATION DEBATE

B. Jefferies

2020

In a debate as crucial and heated as the matter of ordaining women to the priesthood in the Anglican Church in North America, it is worth trying to understand what motivates the other side. In my case, being convinced that the received catholic interpretation of the Scriptures is definitive, the "other side" commends and supports the ordination of women to the priesthood.

HOW CAN I ACCOUNT FOR THE VIEWS ON THE "OTHER SIDE"?

Due to the diversity of parties and traditions within Anglicanism, churchmanship is a large part of the question, sure. But, at the end of the day, we are all Christians reading God's authoritative Word. I believe the "other side" holds their beliefs in good faith. They are every bit as educated and wise as the scholars on "my side". For the most part, we use the same interpretive tools to unpack the meaning of Scripture. "They" desire to honor and obey the Living God every bit as much as "us".

How then, do they come to such opposite conclusions on this question? While the dominance of Gender Studies in the Academy cannot be fully excluded from the equation—it is in the very air that we breathe now—I believe there is an additional factor that might come to bear as motivation: The failure of male clergy.

Since I am myself a male priest in the ACNA, this means a failure that I am party to.

Brothers, we have failed.
We have failed in how we have carried the ministry of priesthood.

If we had carried our ministries in a more apostolic, more Christ-like fashion, perhaps the wider Church, against the winds of change, would have rested more content in her inheritance of an all-male priesthood. Perhaps there would be less of a felt need to admit women to the priesthood, had we male priests done our job better. Brothers, I believe we have failed.

HOW HAVE WE FAILED, EXACTLY?

We have failed:

When we have blurred the boundaries between a God-given holy male-headship and a simplistic cultural patriarchalism.

When we used "ministry" and "ordained ministry" as synonyms, thus relegating true, Spirit-filled ministry that could be done by lay men or women to a second-tier incidental in the life of the Church.

When we accepted worldly accolade, glory, or perks for being an ordained minister, thus socially allowing the order to be seen as superior, rather than that of a servant.

When we have—in word, deed, or allowance—given credence to the false idea that an ordained minister is somehow a special sort of human being.

When we have failed to rightly magnify the gift that is the property of all baptized Christians: The Indwelling Spirit of God.

When we have neglected the public reading of Scripture, and have not brought forward the full witness of the New Testament, including 1 Timothy 2, for the people of God to mark and inwardly digest.

When, despite the clear teaching of the Bible that (1) men and women equally are made in the Image of God and (2) the distinction of "male and female" is of no consequence in Christ (Gal 3:28), we have nevertheless taught or implied that women are in any way ontically inferior to men.

When we, out of resistance to women in the priesthood, have discouraged or prohibited women from exercising their rightful and biblically-sanctioned ministries:

Catechist (cf. Priscilla),
Teacher (cf. Euodia and Syntyche),
Small-Group Leader (cf. The female prophets in 1 Cor. 11),
Lector and Deaconess (cf. Phoebe), and
Lay Eucharistic Minister (cf. Mary, bearer of our Lord).

When we have thought that some members of the body are of greater value than others, or allowed others to believe the same, arrogantly asserting that the eye is more important than the hand.

When we have laughed at jokes about women, Or worse, when we have made them ourselves, perhaps even from the pulpit.

When we have been weak and two-faced, not confronting sin and dysfunction in the church head-on but allowing others to suffer.

When we have equated machismo with manliness, and have been pushy, bossy, rude, harsh or condescending, all under the ruse of "strong leadership."

When we have seen inordinate emotional responses and the need for psychotherapy in ourselves, and have not gone to a therapist.

When we have adopted a "father knows best" approach and not humbly accepted the counsel of others.

When we have not sought to truly love our congregations from the heart, and instead have grumbled against them to others.

When we have tried to further our own convictions with a "thus saith the Lord."

When we have bowed down to the capitalist idol of over-work, and clocked too many hours "for the Church", robbing our families of the debt of love we owe to them.

When we have equated cultural expressions of manliness with godly expressions, and made men who don't like sports or hiking to feel like they are less manly for the fact.

When we have preached things that we do not do ourselves.

When we have engaged with other Christians who support the ordination of women to the priesthood with contempt, anger, slander, malice, or scorn.

In short, when we have not been good fathers, we have failed. It's not the only reason, to be sure, but I believe part of why so many in the church today want "mothers" is because the fathers have so often failed us. As Christians we want—we desperately need—someone who will take care of our souls, and many fathers have made a mess of it, myself included.

So, apart from all debate, I'm calling out to all spiritual fathers: Play the man. Join me in crying out to God to make us servants to the church like St. Paul was a servant. Fast for yourselves and for the brothers.

And if you recognize any traits from my lament in your own ministry (and I hate to say: I recognize some of them in myself)—repent.

Cry out with me to our heavenly Father, to pour out his fatherly gifts into our hearts, that we may carry out the ministry of his Son in a manner more in keeping with him who humbled himself, taking on the likeness of a servant. If we men can do better, with God's help, maybe the church won't feel the need to ask Eve to stand in for Adam at the altar.

As C.S. Lewis so memorably put it in his 1948 essay *Priestesses in the Church?*, "We men may often make very bad priests. That is because we are insufficiently masculine. It is no cure to call in those who are not masculine at all. A given man may make a very bad husband; you cannot mend matters by trying to reverse the roles. He may make a bad male partner in a dance. The cure for that is that men should more diligently attend dancing classes; not that the ballroom should henceforward ignore distinctions of sex and treat all dancers as neuter."

If we male priests inhabited the priesthood with more modesty and gentleness and humility, then it would be more apparent to the wider church that indeed, a priest is only one of many roles within the church that is necessary for her life and health.

If we carried our priesthood in a more Christ-like manner, it would cease to appear as something desirable, something to be grasped, something that was necessary for the real equality of the sexes in the Kingdom of God to be on display.

Consider how different it was in St. Paul's time—the Apostles were exhibited as the refuse of the world. No one wanted to be one! And yet they ministered with a godly authority that has been rare ever since. And additionally, in their time, the fullness of ministries, of both men and women, were possible. How many of our churches today would honor a woman who prophesies, the way they were honored in Corinth? How many priests today would say of a woman who serves in the parish, that she is indeed a bona fide co-laborer in the gospel (Cf. Phil 4:2-3)?

Reducing the man-made self-importance of the priesthood is an essential component to the building up of the church, and equitable flourishing of both men and women in her midst.

Brothers, let us repent of our failures.

GOD IS NOT FAIR

G. McDermott

2020

God is not fair. He deprives men of the most profound and satisfying experience imaginable. Both men and women participate in the creation of another human being, but only women get to carry that little human being inside their body for nine months, nourishing that baby with sustenance from their own body. Only women get to bring that precious child into the world. In many cases, that child will have a more intimate relationship with its mother than with anyone else in the world.

So if God believes in equality, it is a different equality from what most think. God's equality does not mean giving every person the same chance to do everything.

Neither did Jesus' equality mean that. He treated women in revolutionary ways, and had female disciples like Mary who studied with him in ways normally impossible for Jewish women. Women traveled with him and talked with him in public in ways that violated cultural conventions. So when

he chose his twelve apostles, it wasn't the culture or his own fears that prevented him from including women.
This is difficult to think through because we want to believe that Jesus must have believed in equality as we do. But he did not.

Nor did Paul. Several times he told wives to be submissive to their husbands. He never told husbands to submit to their wives. Sure, he told the members of the Ephesian church to submit to one another (Eph. 5:21). But then his very next word was for wives to submit to their husbands (Eph. 5:22). At that point, we expect him to follow that up with a word to husbands to submit to their wives, but he does not.

He said women were not to exercise authority (presumably as a pastor in the church) over a man (1 Tim. 2:12). Women—not men—were to have a symbol of authority on their heads (1 Cor. 11:10). A bishop, presbyter, and deacon was—each one of them—to be the husband of one wife (1 Tim. 3:2; 3:12; Titus 1:6).

Was Paul so man-focused because his culture would not permit female religious leaders, and he could never imagine such a thing?

Hardly. The ancient world was full of altars and shrines with priestesses at Rome, Corinth, and every major city. Ephesus was dominated by an enormous temple to Artemis (Diana), led by a female priest and her female assistants. So female presbyters in the early Church would not have been revolutionary. They were all over the Mediterranean world and particularly in the backyard of one of the early Church's most important centers. Yet none of the elders in the church at Ephesus was female (Acts 20:17-38); all the articles and pronouns designating the elders are masculine.

But are we missing something? Is Paul simply talking about our fallen condition, whereas Jesus wants to redeem us from fallenness and bring us to the new creation which recreates things before the fall?

The problem is that Paul argues for male headship based on things before the fall—not after the fall. He says women should not be pastors because "Adam was formed first, then Eve" (1 Tim. 2:13). That is an argument based on the situation before the fall. He told the Corinthians that men don't need to cover their heads because "man was not made from woman, but woman from man. Neither was man created for woman, but woman for man" (1 Cor. 11:8-9). Again, Paul appealed to the situation before the fall.

Perhaps we are revolted by what Paul said and by what Jesus did (or did not do) because they violate what recent cultural mavens have told us. Men and women are absolutely equal in every way, we have been told. Therefore they should have the same role in every sphere of life, and many of us Christians have deduced that they should have the same roles in the Church. After all, didn't Paul himself say that in Christ "there is not male and female" (Gal. 3:28)?

He did indeed. Yet this is in the midst of his passionate argument that we are "justified by faith" (Gal. 3:24) and not "by the law" (Gal. 3:11). In other words, you don't have to be a Jew or a Jewish man who obeys Jewish law to be saved. All that matters is whether you—Jew or gentile, man or woman—give allegiance to the Jewish messiah (Gal. 3:26).

As long as any of these are baptized into that messiah, they have "put on messiah" (Gal. 3:27).

This famous verse—Galatians 3:28—has nothing to do with family or church ministry roles but with salvation through the Jewish messiah. Men and women alike are saved by baptism and faith in that same Jewish messiah, and that has nothing to do with their roles in the home or church.

Paul's point is equality in justification by the Jewish messiah, not equality in roles in the home or church.

We late moderns want to apply Galatians 3:28 to the home and church, but Paul refused to.

That is our conundrum in the ACNA. We want to extend Galatians 3:28 to realms where Paul and Jesus clearly did not go.

What do we do? Should we feel a bit uncomfortable about trying to improve on what Paul and Jesus thought and did?

WOMEN'S ORDINATION: THE WAY BACK

C. Findley

2020

C.S. Lewis once remarked, *"If you are on the wrong road, progress means doing an about-turn and walking back to the right road; and in that case the man who turns back soonest is the most progressive man."* (Mere Christianity)

The debate on Women's Ordination has been ongoing since at least the late 1960's. Since that time numerous committees and sub-groups have studied the issue as well as its sacramental and ecclesiological implications. The most recent statement by the College of Bishops in the Anglican Church in North America said that the ordination of women to the priesthood within the Province did not have sufficient historical or Biblical warrant. If their statement is correct, and I believe it is, then how can we continue walking further down this road? If we, as a Church body, have said that the Scriptures and tradition of the Church do not support this practice, why would we continue it? To defer to the Constitutions and Canons is a side-step of great error which implies that the Constitution and Canons of the Church carry more weight than the Scripture and traditions that have been passed down to us, which all priests and bishops pledged fidelity to at their ordination.

My purpose is not to re-hash already well-done debates. Many minds, far greater than my own, have done excellent work in this area. My purpose is to suggest a way to achieve, as Lewis says, an "about-turn" and how we can walk back to the right road.

IMMEDIATE STEPS

First, we need to recognize the utterly untenable nature of our current position. Currently the idea of "dual-integrities" is the position de-facto of the ACNA. This basically says that those who are for, and active in, ordaining women have arrived at their position through careful study, prayer, and counsel and feel convinced of the Holy Spirit's approval of their actions. This position likewise says, that simultaneously, those who do *not* believe in the ordination of women have arrived at *their* position through careful study, prayer, and counsel and feel convicted of the Holy Spirit's approval of *their* position.

This is logically impossible. Simply put, both positions cannot be correct. Either women are to be ordained into Holy Orders, or they are not. There is no both/and option. These are exclusive positions.

We should also be honest. The notion of Dual-Integrity is not a theological position, but a political strategy. It seeks to try to hold together disparate views on Holy Orders for the sake of brokering a "live-and-let-live" policy that will ostensibly hold together a divided church. It is a theologically bankrupt position.

In their own and unanimously passed statement alluded to above, the College of Bishops said:

> "However, we also acknowledge that this practice [Women's Ordination] is a recent innovation to Apostolic Tradition and Catholic Order. We agree that there is insufficient scriptural warrant to accept women's ordination to the priesthood as standard practice throughout the Province. However, we continue to acknowledge that individual dioceses have constitutional authority to ordain women to the priesthood." (September 2017)

Several questions arise from this statement. Any 'recent innovation' bears the burden of proof to change the currently held position and practice. Yet, so often in these arguments, this principle has been ignored and proponents aim to make those who hold to the historic position prove why women should *not* be ordained to the priesthood. So, has the case been made that the historic apostolic position should be upended? By the Bishop's plain words, no.

The College of Bishops said, *"We agree that there is insufficient scriptural warrant to accept women's ordination to the priesthood…"* and then add the odd qualifying statement, *"as a standard practice throughout the Province."* This then begs the question that if the Bishops agree that this is a.) a recent innovation to Apostolic Tradition and Catholic Order and b.) there is insufficient scriptural warrant to accept women's ordination to the priesthood, then why would it be acceptable as standard practice in *any* diocese of the Province? When and why is it acceptable to go against apostolic tradition, Catholic order and practice, to do something which you have admitted there is no Scriptural warrant?

We are in a difficult situation. Any attempt to do an about-face and get back on the right road is going to be painful. Making a course correction of this sort is not easy. But is it not worth the effort in order to bring us into Biblical and Apostolic order? I believe so.

STEP 1: VOLUNTARY MORATORIUM

Therefore, we need to move from Dual-Integrity to Biblical-Historical integrity. The simplest way to do this would be a voluntary moratorium by the College of Bishops on the practice of ordaining women to Holy Orders.

This is the most obvious way we can stop moving down this self-admitted wrong road. It is within the power of the College of Bishops to call a halt to our ahistorical and unbiblical direction in this matter.

The matter of Canonical appropriateness need not be a hinderance. Bishops always have the discretion to ordain or not ordain any candidate. Simply because the Constitutions and Canons make provision for the practice of ordaining women to Holy Orders does not mean that any Bishop is obligated to do so.

STEP 2: EDUCATION OF THE CHURCH

The next crucial step would be the education, and in some instances, the re-education of the Church. It would be imperative that the College of Bishops, and us as priests of the Church, be patient, yet diligent, in teaching the "why" behind the Bishop's Moratorium. Undoubtedly this would cause much weeping and gnashing of teeth, but Biblical faithfulness often does. After all, it is to such apostolic faithfulness we are called.

This could include, but certainly is not limited to, papers from the College of Bishops, teachings, workshops, and publications designed to teach our laity and clergy the historic understanding not simply of women in the Church, but of Holy Orders in general. The current understanding of Holy Orders and the Priesthood is perhaps the root of the issue, yet perhaps it is better suited at this time as the subject of separate, but related, conversation.

Another facet to this education could be an uplifting of women in ministry, a teaching that demonstrates, particularly from history, the roles women have played in the propagation of the Gospel of Jesus Christ. It would be important to not only teach why only men may be ordained to Holy Orders, and why women may not, but also the understanding that the collar is not the key nor the barrier to effective ministry for Christ in his Church.

When St. John Paul II took a strong stand for the male-only priesthood, he did so in a characteristically pastoral way. He was clear in the Church's conviction of the male-only priesthood and he simultaneously upheld the dignity of womanhood. In the encyclical, "Oridinatio Sacerdotalis" (May, 1994) he said:

> "The fact that the Blessed Virgin Mary, Mother of God and Mother of the Church, received neither the mission proper to the Apostles nor the ministerial priesthood clearly shows that the non-admission of women to priestly ordination cannot mean that women are of lesser dignity, nor can it be construed as discrimination against them. Rather, it is to be seen as the faithful observance of a plan to be ascribed to the wisdom of the Lord of the universe."

A similar approach would seem advisable. It will not be enough to simply state the Church's position. Instead, the call should be for the faithful to contemplate a deep appreciation of women and men and the inherent dignity that is theirs in the Imago Dei.

STEP 3: CURRENT WOMEN IN HOLY ORDERS

Assuming the Bishop's heartfelt conviction on this issue, there remains the uncomfortable question of how to implement this course reversal regarding the women currently in Holy Orders. These are women of faith, no doubt, ministering in the name of the Lord Jesus, who are presently serving in various capacities within the ACNA.

There is no easy solution here. If the Bishops have concluded this is an ahistorical and ultimately unbiblical practice, then this difficult work must be done. This has tremendous application in particular, for the administration of the Sacraments. If this is a wrong move, then it must be corrected decisively. One way to handle this is to revert all women ordained to the priesthood to the Diaconate. This would solve the immediate concern over the administration of the Sacraments. They would be free to continue to exercise their ministry, but within the Order of Deacons.

Regarding women already ordained to the Diaconate, they could continue to serve in this capacity, but the moratorium would also extend to these ordinations as well. There are those who hold that women may hold the office of Deacon, I do not believe that Scripture or the historic practice of the Church supports that position.

STEP 4: RESTORE THE ORDER OF DEACONESSES

A historical and Biblically faithful opportunity to incorporate women into the ministerial life of the Church would be to restore an active and robust Order of Deaconesses. This would be a lay order, set apart and dedicated to service and to the furtherance of the Gospel within the ACNA.

A movement of this sort would need to be implemented with great intention and careful thought. It seems to me, that it would be important to give this office its own duties and responsibilities and dignity. An Order of Deaconesses should not be seen, in any way, as some sort of 'inferior' ministry. Rather it should be seen in light of a sense of "differing gifts" as outlined by St. Paul in Romans 12 and 1 Corinthians 12:12-27.

This ministry should be lifted up and promoted at the Provincial, Diocesan, and Parish levels for women called to serve Christ in this particular way in His Church.

STEP 5: BE DONE WITH THE ENDLESS ARGUMENTS

Finally, I think it will be imperative that we be done with the endless politicking and arguing over this issue. At least two generations, perhaps three, have been caught up in the in-fighting and confusion regarding women in Holy Orders. Strong and decisive leadership will be required to lead the way in this effort.

CONCLUSION

In John Chapter 16, Jesus tells the apostles, "When the Spirit of truth comes, he will guide you into all the truth." (John 16:13, ESV) If we believe that after the multi-year study conducted for the College of Bishops, that we have the Spirit's word on this, then we stand at a critical juncture in the life of the Church. Will we listen and obey?

I have a number of women friends, sisters in Christ, whom I love dearly, that I know will find these ideas very difficult indeed. I understand how personal and precious their ministerial work is to them. And in all this I truly mean no offense to them. However, it should be true for us all, that our greatest concern should be faithfulness to Biblical truth, informed by the Spirit-guided tradition of the Church as understood in Catholic faith and order. But it requires not just the conviction of the truth, but our willingness to be submissive and obedient to it.

My prayer is that the ACNA, all of us, will do just that.

Post-Script
DEACONESSES OR CHOR-DIACONATE?
B. Jefferies

Fr. Findley's proposal for a revival of the order of Deaconess is a solid one. It may however present two difficulties. Many may mistake it as merely the feminine form of the word "Deacon" and assume it is of the same order. It also might be questioned whether the functions of the order of Deaconess (as it was reprised in Anglicanism in the late 19th century) fully encompasses the variety of authorized female ministry witnessed in the NT. For these reasons, I want to suggest that the new creation of a Chor-Diaconate might be a better order for women to minister within.

While a clearly delineated three-fold order of Bishop, Priest, and Deacon is present in the writings of the Apostolic Fathers (those godly men who were discipled by the Apostles themselves), and this order has been maintained for twenty centuries now, as the ordering of the ordained ministry within the catholic Church, nevertheless there are some variations from the rule. There were the so-called "minor-orders" of the middle ages: Sub-deacon, Acolyte, Exorcist, Lector, and Porter. As the Apostles (in Acts chapter 6) created the order of Deacons by partitioning a portion of their own God-given trust to qualified men, so portions of a deacon's ministry were further portioned off into the minor-orders.

From the second through to the twelfth centuries there was an order known as the 'Chor-episcopi' or "country-bishops". A priest who was ordained as a Chor-bishop was given authority to confirm but was not given authority to ordain, like a "full" bishop. These chor-bishops inhabited a ministry somewhere between the Suffragan-Bishop and the diocesan Dean of today.

These variations from the standard three-fold order teach us two things about Holy Orders: One, that all ordering descends from the Bishop. All ordained ministry is given authority to do a portion of the ministry entrusted to the Bishop, but only the Bishop, as heir to the Apostles, has the authority to do all of the acts of ordained ministry, inclusive of ordaining other ministers. Two, from time to time, as circumstance demanded, there could be certain "halfway" orderings, that work within and compliment the three-fold order: A chor-bishop is "halfway" between a bishop and a priest. A sub-deacon is "halfway" between a deacon and a laic.

This understanding creates a backdrop in which a future of women in ministry in the Anglican Church in North America can be discerned. A future in which the Biblical mandates are obeyed, the catholic tradition received, and the women who have experienced a call to ministry can inhabit and flourish in the calling. The solution: Chor-deacons. Let the ACNA create the order of Chor-deacon, and consider all women presently ordained to the priesthood or diaconate to have a portion of that ordering stand, the portion allotted to the Chor-deacon. In the same way that a Chor-bishop was given all the authority of a Bishop except the authority to ordain, a Chor-deacon would be given all the authority of a deacon except the authority to lead a congregation (e.g. as a "Deacon-in-charge") and by extension, to be the authoritative preaching voice within a congregation. A Chor-deacon may preach on occasion, but not as the regular preacher, since that would entail teaching-with-authority over men, which is prohibited by 1 Tim 2:12. It might also serve (at the level of symbolism) if Chor-deacons preached from the chancel-step, rather than from the pulpit, and refrained from beginning their sermons with the customary triune invocation, thus further re-enforcing the intended distinction.

A Chor-deacon would be slightly "more" than a "Deaconess" (as that title is used in the Apostolic Traditions, and in the early 20th century revival of that order), but slightly "less" than a full deacon.

It occupies a similar ambiguity as the chor-bishops did long ago, but meets a most practical need and very real constraint: The need to honor the call women experience into ordained ministry, and the constraint of catholic ecumenical consensus. A Chor-Deacon would be ordained using the Liturgy for an Ordination of a Deacon in the Book of Common Prayer, with just two amendments: The omission of the words "and preach" in the Exhortation (BCP 2019, pg. 478, line 2) and the alteration of the word "Deacon" to be "Chor-Deacon" at the time of the imposition of hands (BCP 2019, pg. 480).